Blockchain Security from the Bottom Up

Blockchain Security from the Bottom Up

Securing and Preventing Attacks on Cryptocurrencies, Decentralized Applications, NFTs, and Smart Contracts

Howard E. Poston III

WILEY

To Dad, Mom, Brit, Jon, Rachel, and all of my family and friends.
Thank you for your love, support, and everything you do.

Acknowledgments

Thanks to the amazing team at Wiley and everyone who encouraged me over the years to write this book. Without you, this book would not have been possible.

About the Author

Howard E. Poston III is a freelance consultant and content creator with a focus on blockchain and cybersecurity. He has developed and taught many courses exploring and explaining various aspects of cybersecurity and has written hundreds of articles on the subject for different outlets. Howard is also the author of several academic articles on security topics and has spoken on blockchain and cybersecurity at international security conferences. In his free time, he enjoys reading, hiking, and working in the garden.

About the Technical Editor

David Hoelzer has been working in the field of information security since the early 1990s. While he consults or has served as a chief information security officer (CISO) and enterprise security architect, he is also highly technical, having built a variety of blockchain tools used both for transaction management and for identifying and tracking transaction patterns. His primary knowledge area is in the arena of network security, monitoring, and forensics. His current focus is applied research developing deep learning solutions to automate and accelerate anomaly detection and security operations. David is a Fellow with the SANS Institute, where he has taught since 1999. He is also the Dean of Faculty and a board member at STI.edu, a graduate school offering master's degrees and graduate certificates in applied information security.

Contents at a Glance

Contents

Blockchain Security from the Bottom Up

Introduction to Blockchain Security

Blockchain is a new and exciting technology that provides alternative ways of accomplishing common goals. Blockchains make it possible to maintain distributed, decentralized, and immutable digital ledgers. The contents of these ledgers are also designed to be publicly visible, enabling anyone in the blockchain network to independently verify the legitimacy of the data and transactions that the ledgers contain.

However, blockchain technology is also complex. Even the original, basic blockchains like Bitcoin are multilayered systems that use an array of algorithms to ensure the validity and immutability of the distributed ledger. Smart contract platforms go even further, allowing programs to run on top of the distributed ledger.

Before diving into blockchain security and how these systems can be attacked, an understanding of some fundamentals is necessary. This chapter starts with a discussion of the goals of the blockchain and how it works at a high level. In the second half, I'll break down the blockchain ecosystem into more manageable chunks and discuss threat modeling for the blockchain.

The Goals of Blockchain Technology

Blockchain technology provides an alternative means of maintaining a digital ledger. The design of the blockchain offers certain promises or guarantees that are fulfilled at varying levels.

Anonymity

One of the biggest promises of blockchain technology is anonymity. Blockchain-based systems are designed to tie asset ownership and transaction creation to an address rather than a real-world identity. Since account addresses are based on public/private keys that are randomly generated, which in theory should provide a level of anonymity.

In reality, though, blockchain technology provides pseudonymity, not anonymity. By collecting publicly available information from the blockchain's distributed ledger, it may be possible to infer information about an account owner, breaking anonymity.

Decentralization

One of the primary objectives of blockchain technology is to create a distributed, decentralized digital ledger system. In the past, maintaining a single, official ledger required a centralized authority or group. Blockchain technology uses consensus algorithms, cryptographic primitives, and other tools to replace this central authority.

Most blockchain systems are not as decentralized as intended. Blockchain consensus algorithms tend to encourage centralization. For example, Proof of Work miners tend to form pools to guarantee more consistent rewards, and with the Proof of Stake consensus algorithm, the rich get richer and more able to control the blockchain over time.

Fault Tolerance

Resiliency and fault tolerance are vital features for an IT system. On multiple occasions, the failure of a single critical component has knocked a company or a significant portion of the Internet offline.

Blockchain systems are inherently fault tolerant because of their decentralization. Theoretically, no node in the blockchain network is essential to its operation, and the network can continue to operate—with greatly reduced performance and security—if only a single node remains online. However, as blockchains become more centralized, disruptions are easier to accomplish and with higher impact.

Immutability

Blockchains are designed to create an immutable, decentralized distributed ledger. Each node in the blockchain network is responsible for maintaining its own copy of the distributed ledger.

If each node maintains its own copy of the ledger, some mechanism needs to exist to prevent them from making changes to their copies of the ledger. The blockchain uses hash functions, digital signatures, and other algorithms to make it infeasible to forge blocks and make changes to the ledger that would be accepted by the rest of the network.

Transparency

Centralized systems for maintaining ledgers are generally not very transparent. For example, the internal processes of a bank are very opaque, making it difficult to determine how fairly it maintains its internal ledger. As a result, customers need to trust the bank to behave fairly and in their best interest in order to give banks their business.

In contrast, the blockchain implements a very transparent digital ledger. All nodes in the blockchain network are responsible for maintaining a copy of the ledger and validating all blocks before including them in the ledger. This transparency allows anyone to verify the validity of any transaction on the blockchain ledger.

Trustless

As mentioned, traditional systems for maintaining a ledger required trust in a centralized authority. Blockchain is designed to eliminate this need for trust while still maintaining a trusted ledger.

Blockchain systems accomplish this to some degree by using Byzantine Fault Tolerant consensus algorithms to maintain a decentralized digital ledger. Byzantine Fault Tolerant algorithms are resistant against a certain number of traitors, eliminating the need for blockchain nodes to trust in one another. This resistance is augmented by algorithms that reward users for acting honestly and in the best interests of the blockchain.

Structure of the Blockchain

The blockchain is a complex, multilayered environment. Figure 1.1 shows a drill-down from the blockchain network to the contents of a single transaction.

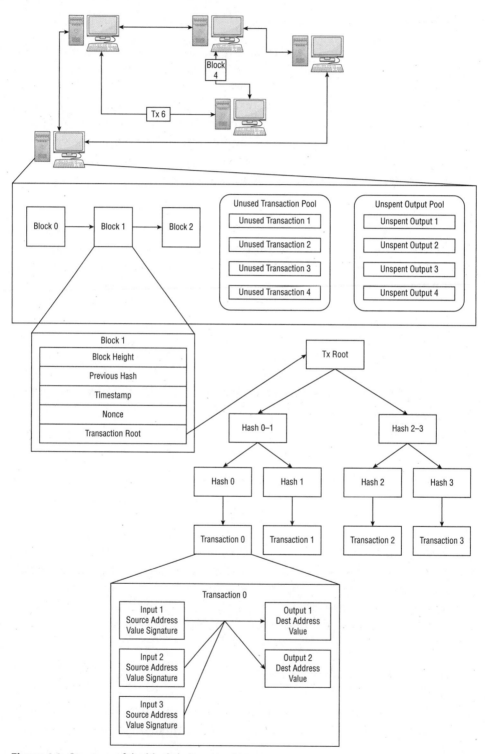

Figure 1.1: Structure of the blockchain ecosystem

The complexity of the blockchain network can make this figure difficult to read and understand. In the following sections, I'll break it down into its component parts.

The Blockchain Network

The blockchain is designed to create a distributed, decentralized digital ledger. This ledger is maintained by a network of blockchain nodes as shown in Figure 1.2.

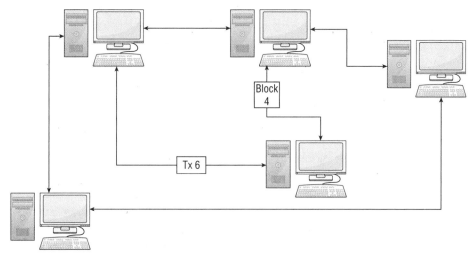

Figure 1.2: Structure of the blockchain network

The blockchain network uses a peer-to-peer network to communicate. Each node in the network is connected to only a few neighbors that they directly communicate with.

Transactions and blocks sent out over the network propagate across via multiple hops. Each node in the network can then store and process the transactions for inclusion in a new block and blocks it receives for inclusion in its copy of the distributed ledger.

The Blockchain Node

Blockchain's decentralization means that each blockchain node is responsible for performing all of the operations that make the blockchain work. Figure 1.3 illustrates some of the key components.

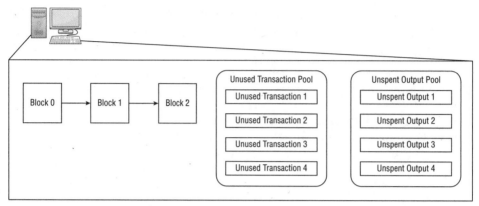

Figure 1.3: Structure of a blockchain block

Each node in the blockchain network is responsible for maintaining and updating a complete copy of the digital ledger, which consists of a chain of blocks. The node must store the full blockchain and may also maintain a more accessible version. For example, Ethereum maintains a database of the current state that is derived from and updated by the blockchain and reflects the current state of the blockchain.

Additionally, a node may be involved in the process of creating new blocks. This requires knowledge of transactions that have not yet been included in blocks and the outputs of previous transactions that could be used in new transactions. For example, these unused outputs may describe the current allocation of a blockchain's cryptocurrency.

A blockchain node may also have other responsibilities beyond maintaining the basic blockchain. For example, smart contract platforms are designed to create a decentralized computer. For this to work, each node will also host a virtual machine (VM) in which instructions (contained in transactions) will be executed as each new block is added to the blockchain.

A Blockchain Block

Blocks are the fundamental components of the blockchain. As shown in Figure 1.4, a blockchain block is composed of two main parts.

The block header, shown on the left in Figure 1.4, is the portion of the block that actually is part of the blockchain. Each block header contains metadata about a block, including the root hash of the block's Merkle tree.

Block headers are chained together using hash functions, with each block header containing the hash of the previous block. Hash functions are collision-resistant, meaning that it is infeasible to find two inputs that produce the same hash output. By including the previous block hash in each block header, the blockchain makes it infeasible to change one block without also changing every block following it. This makes it much more difficult to forge blocks and attempt to rewrite the history of the distributed ledger. The body of a block contains a list of the transactions within that block. While these transactions may be communicated as a list, they are designed to be organized into a Merkle tree as shown on the right in Figure 1.4.

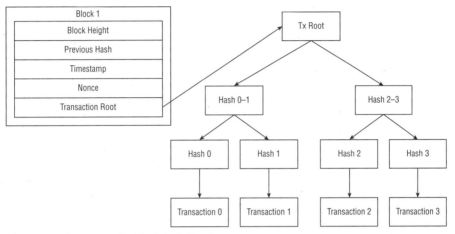

Figure 1.4: Structure of a blockchain block

In a Merkle tree, the leaf nodes contain the hashes of transactions, and all internal nodes contain the hash of their two children. Due to the properties of hash functions, this structure makes it infeasible to find two versions of a Merkle tree (of a particular size) that have the same root hash value. As a result, the single root hash contained within the block header securely summarizes the list of transactions and grants them the protection of blockchain immutability.

A Blockchain Transaction

The original blockchain, Bitcoin, was designed to be a cryptocurrency. The blockchain's distributed ledger was intended to record the transfers of Bitcoin between various accounts.

For this reason, the data stored on the blockchain's digital ledger are called transactions. Figure 1.5 shows an example of a blockchain transaction.

The name *transaction* is a bit misleading because a blockchain transaction can include multiple transfers of value between different accounts. Figure 1.5 shows transfers of the same cryptocurrency, where all inputs are pooled before being allocated to outputs; however, a transaction can also include multiple transfers of distinct tokens or independent actions.

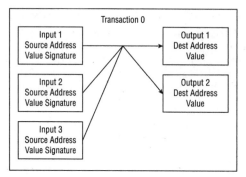

Figure 1.5: Structure of a blockchain transaction

At a minimum, an input to a blockchain transaction must contain a source address, amount, and digital signature. These fields describe the purpose of the transaction and demonstrate that it was authorized by someone with access to the private key associated with the account (ideally the account owner). Additionally, a transaction input must be valid, which often means that it is an unused output of another transaction.

Most blockchains do not require transactions to be authorized by the recipient, so they must include only an address and an amount. If a transaction is valid, its outputs can be used by their recipients as inputs to new transactions.

Inside the Blockchain Ecosystem

As mentioned earlier, blockchain environments are complex and multilayered. Cyberattacks and security vulnerabilities can exist at multiple layers of the blockchain ecosystem, and attackers can achieve the same goals in multiple different ways.

When discussing blockchain security, it can be helpful to break the blockchain ecosystem into a few different layers. This book will explore four different layers of the blockchain with two sublayers within each layer.

Fundamentals

The goal of the blockchain is to maintain a distributed digital ledger while eliminating the need for a trusted, centralized authority. Instead, each node in the network maintains a copy of the ledger that it updates in sync with the rest of the network. To accomplish this goal, the blockchain relies heavily on cryptographic primitives and defines certain data structures for storing and communicating the information stored on the distributed ledger.

Primitives

Distributed ledger technology is built on cryptography. One of the major goals of blockchain is to transfer the requirement for trust from a centralized authority to cryptographic and other algorithms.

Cryptographic primitives, such as hash functions and public key cryptography, provide vital security guarantees for the blockchain. Between them, hash functions and public key cryptography can ensure confidentiality, integrity, and authentication for data.

These primitives are used throughout the blockchain for a variety of different purposes, which makes their security vital for blockchain security. If the security of hash functions or public key cryptography is broken due to compromised keys, algorithmic vulnerabilities, and so on, the blockchain falls apart.

Data Structures

The purpose of the blockchain is to create a distributed, immutable digital ledger. A core part of this role is data storage.

Information is stored in the ledger in a specific format, which may vary from implementation to implementation. If the way that data is stored opens the system to attack, it can affect the security of the data stored in the ledger.

Protocols

Distributed ledger systems are defined as set protocols rather than specific implementations. Like the web protocol, HTTP, client software designed by different vendors can interact as long as they follow the set rules of the protocol. While blockchains can have implementation errors that create security issues, a blockchain protocol may also be vulnerable to theoretical attacks.

A 51% attack on a Proof of Work blockchain is an example of such a protocol-level attack. This type of attack is an acknowledged risk in the design of a Proof of Work blockchain and takes advantage of how security and decentralization are enforced within the system.

Consensus

Blockchains are designed to create a shared, distributed digital ledger. Each node in the blockchain network independently maintains and updates its own copy of the ledger. For this to work, these nodes require the ability to synchronize their updates and reach consensus on the current state of the digital ledger.

Blockchain consensus algorithms make it possible for blockchain nodes to agree on the ledger's contents in a trustless environment, assuming that a certain percentage of the blockchain's nodes are honest. Exploiting consensus is necessary for attacks designed to modify the contents of the blockchain's distributed ledger, which is why the 51% attack is the most well-known blockchain attack. This attack takes advantage of the fact that Proof of Work implements a majority vote, and if the attacker controls the majority, they can force the network to accept any valid version of the blockchain that they want.

Block Creation

The blockchain has a defined process for adding new information to the distributed ledger. After creation, transactions are distributed to all blockchain nodes via the peer-to-peer network. Block creators periodically collect transactions into blocks containing these transactions and distribute these blocks to the rest of the network. Nodes then validate these blocks and add them to their copies of the distributed ledger.

This process leaves multiple opportunities for disruption or for an attacker to take advantage. For example, an attacker who identifies the selected creator of the next block could perform a distributed denial-of-service (DDoS) attack against that node to delay or prevent the creation of a block.

Infrastructure

The concept of the blockchain was initially defined theoretically in the Bitcoin white paper. However, to be useful, the blockchain needs to be implemented using modern technology.

A few months after the release of the Bitcoin white paper, Satoshi Nakamoto released the first implementation of the Bitcoin software. This and other blockchain software run on nodes and communicate over the network.

Nodes

Distributed ledger systems are implemented as software that runs on a user's computer. This software interacts with the user, other software on the computer, and the computer's operating system and core functionality (memory management, network stack, etc.).

An attacker can use malware and other techniques to attack the security of the blockchain at this level. For example, malware may be used to steal the private key associated with a blockchain account or to perform a denial-of-service attack to prevent a node from building a block or updating its copy of the ledger.

Network

Blockchain nodes communicate using a peer-to-peer network to send transactions and blocks to one another. These peer-to-peer communications occur over traditional network infrastructure such as the public Internet or an internal enterprise network.

These communications are vital to ensuring that the blockchain achieves consensus and that nodes have access to the latest transactions and blocks. An attacker who can disrupt these communications can perform a DoS attack on the network or facilitate other attacks. For example, an attack that breaks the blockchain network into isolated fragments can make a 51% easier and less expensive to perform.

Advanced

The original Bitcoin blockchain was designed to implement a decentralized financial system that tracked ownership and transfers of the Bitcoin cryptocurrency. Over time, the purpose and functions of blockchain have expanded. Today, many blockchains support execution of smart contracts on top of the blockchain or enable integration of blockchain software with external applications.

Smart Contracts

Smart contract platforms are blockchains designed to allow programs to run on top of the distributed ledger. Blockchain nodes host a virtual machine and execute instructions contained within blockchain transactions.

Smart contracts introduce new security risks and means by which a blockchain can be attacked. Vulnerable smart contracts can cause harm to themselves, their users, or the blockchain network as a whole.

Extensions

Distributed ledger systems are often not designed to be self-contained. External applications can connect to the system via the built-in API or through smart contracts running on the platform.

These extensions are part of the system's threat surface and potentially allow an attacker to compromise the security of the blockchain and vice versa.

For example, exploitation of a vulnerable system that holds blockchain private keys could allow an attacker to perform transactions on the user's behalf.

Threat Modeling for the Blockchain

Threat modeling is an exercise designed to help with identifying potential security threats to a system. By using a defined threat modeling framework, security researchers can better target their investigations and decrease the probability of potential oversights.

In this book, I'll use the STRIDE threat model to explore blockchain security threats. This model, combined with the various blockchain layers discussed previously, helps to clarify the discussion of various blockchain security threats.

Threat Modeling with STRIDE

STRIDE is a mnemonic created by Microsoft employees to help with identification and classification of potential threats to a system. The letters in STRIDE stand for spoofing, tampering, repudiation, information disclosure, denial of service, and elevation of privilege.

While STRIDE was designed for traditional IT environments, it can also be mapped to the blockchain. Each of the six threat classes applies to the blockchain as well.

Spoofing

Spoofing refers to attacks that threaten the authenticity of data within the system. If an attacker can masquerade as a legitimate user within the system, the security of the system could be damaged.

In a blockchain system, the primary way in which a user interacts with the blockchain is by creating transactions. A spoofing attack in a blockchain environment would involve generating fake transactions that pass validation and digital signature checks.

Tampering

Tampering attacks involve modifying stored data. This could include deleting or changing stored data.

Distributed ledger technology uses hash functions and digital signatures to help maintain the integrity of the ledger at different levels. An attack on the security of the digital signature or hash function is an example of tampering within a blockchain environment.

Repudiation

Repudiation, or more accurately non-repudiation, addresses a user's ability to deny taking an action. Protection against repudiation requires strong authentication and the ability to accurately attribute actions to a particular user.

On the blockchain, repudiation deals with the ability of a user of the distributed ledger to deny that they took certain actions, such as generating and signing a transaction. With asymmetric cryptography, only someone with knowledge of a private key can generate a valid digital signature, making it difficult to deny actions (assuming that the key is properly protected).

Information Disclosure

Information disclosure addresses unauthorized access to sensitive information. In traditional IT environments, this threat is prevented through the use of access controls and data encryption.

While most data is publicly visible on the ledger, some level of privacy can be achieved using a private ledger or encryption of data in the ledger. If an attacker can gain access to a private ledger or steal a private key to decrypt data, sensitive information may be leaked.

Denial of Service

Denial-of-service attacks are designed to degrade or destroy a system's ability to perform its function and respond to legitimate requests. In traditional IT environments, a DDoS attack is the most famous form of this threat and attempts to overwhelm a system with fake, spam requests.

Blockchain systems are designed to be distributed and decentralized, which should provide strong protection against DoS attacks. However, DoS attacks can occur at every level of the distributed ledger implementation. Any attack that makes the system unusable or decreases its efficiency or effectiveness is a DoS attack.

Elevation of Privilege

Privilege escalation refers to an attacker gaining access to protected functionality without the appropriate authorization. With distributed ledger technology, there are several different levels of unauthorized access that an attacker can gain, including at the account, blockchain, and smart contract level.

An attacker should not have access to a legitimate user's account on the distributed ledger system. If an unauthorized user is able to access an account, this is an example of an account-level escalation of privilege.

Most attacks on distributed ledger systems are designed to gain an elevated level of control over the distributed ledger. For example, a 51% attack allows an attacker to rewrite the history of the ledger to meet their needs.

Smart contracts are programs that run on the distributed ledger and are often designed to have protected functionality not accessible to the general public. Vulnerabilities in the smart contract code or a failure to take the system environment into account when designing the smart contract can allow an attacker to gain access to this protected functionality.

Applying STRIDE to Blockchain

The various threats described by the STRIDE threat model can occur at different levels of the blockchain ecosystem. For example, privilege escalation can be accomplished by stealing a user's private key, performing a 51% attack against consensus, or gaining unauthorized access to a smart contract. These are three very different threats that all fall under the same STRIDE category.

In this book, I'll discuss threats and attacks as a combination of the level of the blockchain ecosystem and the associated STRIDE threat. This clarifies the potential threats and impacts of an attack. For example, a 51% attack is an attack against consensus algorithms that could lead to modification of the distributed ledger, which not only breaks the integrity of the ledger but allows an attacker to delete past transactions from the record (repudiation).

Conclusion

Blockchain technology is complex and multilayered, which makes blockchain security a complicated topic as well. Blockchain systems face a variety of different threats at various levels of the blockchain ecosystem.

This chapter broke the blockchain into four layers and eight sublayers and discussed how the STRIDE threat model can be mapped to the blockchain. The next four chapters of this book will explore each of these layers individually and discuss the potential security threats to each level of the blockchain ecosystem.

Fundamentals

The goal of blockchain technology is to create a shared, decentralized digital ledger. In this system, no centralized authority exists to dictate what the official version of the digital ledger is.

Blockchain technology transfers trust in the digital ledger away from a centralized authority to a set of protocols designed to provide the same guarantees as a centralized ledger. These protocols are created using smaller building blocks with certain properties that can provide these desired guarantees.

This chapter explores the fundamentals of blockchain security. This includes the cryptographic primitives and the data structures that are used to build blockchain protocols and make the decentralized digital ledger possible.

Cryptographic Primitives

Financial institutions maintain an internal accounts ledger, enabling value to be transferred from one party to another by simply updating the relevant values in this ledger. Each financial institution is responsible for maintaining the accuracy of its ledger, and customers must trust the financial institution to properly track their financial transactions.

Blockchain is designed to transfer this trust from these centralized authorities to cryptographic algorithms and protocols. The cryptographic algorithms are relied upon to ensure the authenticity and integrity of the transactions recorded on the blockchain's ledger.

Blockchain technology began with Bitcoin, and since then, many different blockchains have emerged, each with its own tweaks on the underlying protocols and methods of implementing them. However, all of these protocols are reliant on the same set of cryptographic building blocks.

The design of the blockchain makes data integrity and authenticity protections vital for the system to work. To provide these protections, blockchain technology uses public key cryptography and hash functions.

Public Key Cryptography

Cryptographic algorithms are divided into two main categories based on how they use encryption keys. Symmetric algorithms use a single key for both encryption and decryption. This symmetry means that the algorithms are generally more efficient, making them better suited for bulk data transfer. However, they require the shared secret key to be distributed to all participants via a secure channel.

Asymmetric, or public key, cryptography uses a public key for encryption and a private key for decryption. This makes it possible to send a secret message to anyone without setting up a shared secret key. However, these algorithms are generally less efficient than their symmetric counterparts.

Blockchain technology is heavily dependent on public key cryptography. Its use of two related keys and the ability to create and validate digital signatures using them provides the invaluable ability to authenticate the sender of a message.

Introducing "Hard" Mathematical Problems

Public key cryptography is built using "hard" mathematical problems. These mathematical functions are defined by an asymmetric relationship between how hard they are to perform versus how hard they are to reverse. For these problems, F(x) has polynomial complexity, while $F^{-1}(x)$ has exponential complexity.

This relationship makes it possible to develop cryptographic algorithms that are both usable and secure. The algorithms are designed so that a legitimate user only has to perform the easy operation, F(x), while any attacker must solve the harder problem, $F^{-1}(x)$.

Several of these mathematically "hard" problems exist. The two most commonly used in "classical" (i.e., not post-quantum) cryptography are the factoring problem, which is the basis for RSA, and the discrete logarithm problem, which is the basis for the Digital Signature Algorithm (DSA). Algorithms based on these problems can also be implemented more efficiently using elliptic curve cryptography (ECC).

The Factoring Problem

In the factoring problem, the easier operation is multiplying two prime numbers. The complexity of doing so is polynomial in the length of the two numbers. This means that an increase in the length of the two primes, such as switching from 128 to 129 bits, has a relatively small impact on the overall complexity.

Factoring inverts multiplication, and factoring has exponential complexity in the length of the factors. The reason for this is that the best-known way to factor two numbers on a non-quantum computer has exponential complexity.

While one of the factors is guaranteed to be less than the square root of the quotient, this is a large space that grows rapidly. Adding a single bit to the length of the primes (i.e., from 128 to 129 bits) doubles the number of potential factors that an attacker needs to search.

The difficulty of factoring grows much faster than the difficulty of multiplying. As a result, it is possible to find a length of these factors where multiplication is possible but factoring is not.

The Discrete Logarithm Problem

The discrete logarithm problem is another asymmetric problem commonly used in public key cryptography. It is based on the "easy" problem of exponentiation and the "hard" problem of logarithms.

As with the factoring problem, the discrete logarithm problem is designed to ensure that legitimate operations are easy compared to malicious ones. Increasing the size of the exponent has a minimal impact on a legitimate user—but a significant impact on an attacker. As with the factoring problem, the best way to solve the discrete logarithm is by guessing possible values for the exponent, so a user can achieve an arbitrary level of security by increasing the key length.

Elliptic Curve Cryptography

Elliptic curve cryptography (ECC) is a type of public key cryptography that uses points on an elliptic curve instead of integers as the basis for computation. An elliptic curve is a mathematical function of the form $y^2 = x^3 + ax + b$.

Using points on these curves as public keys, it's possible to create a public key cryptosystem that uses the same principles as the discrete logarithm problem. On an elliptic curve, an operation called point addition is equivalent to multiplication over the integers, and point multiplication is equivalent to exponentiation.

In elliptic curve cryptography, public keys are derived from private keys by multiplying a random integer (the private key) with a publicly known point on the curve (the generator). As with the factoring and discrete logarithm problems, point addition and multiplication (the equivalents of multiplication and exponentiation) are "easy" for legitimate users, while point subtraction and division (the equivalents of factoring and logarithms) are "hard" for an attacker.

Elliptic curve cryptography has two main advantages over integer-based public key cryptography: key length and energy consumption. Elliptic curve cryptography accomplishes the same level of security as cryptosystems using the discrete logarithm problem with much shorter keys. For example, a 2048-bit RSA key has equivalent security to a 160-bit ECC curve. ECC is also better than algorithms like RSA in low-power environments because the operations used in ECC-based cryptography (point addition and multiplication) consume less power than the equivalent operations over the integers (multiplication and exponentiation).

Building Cryptography with "Hard" Problems

Public key cryptography uses these "hard" problems to build algorithms that are both usable and secure. The design of these algorithms is intended to allow a legitimate user to only perform "easy" operations, while attackers are forced to complete "hard" ones.

A critical part of this process is the derivation of the public/private keypair. While a private key is a random number, the public key is derived from it to have certain properties. The intent is for one key to undo what the other does for a particular algorithm.

For example, the RSA encryption operation is $c = m^e \pmod n$, where c is the ciphertext, m is the message, e is the public key, and n is a public modulus value. Substituting some values in, $2^5 \pmod{14} = 4$.

RSA uses the same operation for decryption, so the private key is selected to undo the effects of encryption. A private key of 11 produces $4^{11} \pmod{14} = 2$.

In the case of RSA, the public and private keys, e and d, are selected so that $m^{d*e} = 1 \pmod{14}$ for any message m, since this is equivalent to the two-stage process that we performed due to the properties of exponents. With a random private key of 11, d had to be 5, according to Euler's totient function.

Since the recipient of the message knows the private key, they can undo the encryption with an exponentiation operation. However, an attacker lacking knowledge of this key would need to calculate a logarithm, which is much harder.

How the Blockchain Uses Public Key Cryptography

Public key cryptographic algorithms can provide confidentiality, integrity, and authentication protections. They are a fundamental part of how the blockchain works and are used for digital signatures and account addressing.

Digital Signatures

In the previous sections, we explored how public key cryptography can be used to protect confidentiality by demonstrating that a private key can be used to create an encrypted message that only the intended recipient can read. Digital signatures flip this around, creating a digital signature that only the alleged sender could generate.

As mentioned, public and private keys are selected so that one undoes what the other does. In the case of RSA, this meant that m^{d*e} = 1 (mod n).

However, it also means that m^{e*d} = 1 (mod n) or that we could "encrypt" with a private key to generate a digital signature and "decrypt" with a public key to get the original plaintext. By generating a signature and sending it alongside the associated data, we can prove that the data could only have been generated by someone who knows the private key and has not been modified in transit. Anyone with access to the associated public key can then "decrypt" the signature and validate that the plaintext matches.

Blockchain uses digital signatures to prove the authenticity of transactions on the blockchain. If cryptocurrency is being transferred out of a particular account, we want to be sure that the transfer was performed by the owner of the account.

Also, we're relying on a peer-to-peer network to carry the transaction and nodes to store copies of it in a pool of unused transactions until it is included in a block. Digital signatures also prove that a transaction has not been modified in transit.

Account Addressing

One of the hard problems associated with digital signatures is proving that a particular public key belongs to a particular user. If an attacker intercepts a message and a signature, they could modify the message, sign it with their own key, and send their own public key alongside it. If the recipient accepts the public key as belonging to the alleged sender, they can validate the signature.

Blockchain solves this problem by using public keys to derive account addresses. This makes it possible to verify that a public key belongs to a particular account by rederiving the account address from the key and checking that it matches.

Security Assumptions of Public Key Cryptography

For public key cryptography to be effective, it needs to be secure. Public key cryptography has two main security assumptions: that both the user's private key and the algorithm used are secure.

Private Key Security

In public key cryptography, the only secret is a user's private key. Anyone with access to this private key can decrypt a message sent to the user or generate a digital signature on their behalf.

A private key must be securely generated and protected throughout its life cycle. If a private key is generated using a weak random number generator or derived from a password or passphrase that is guessable, an attacker may be able to learn the private key. Blockchain security depends on private keys being generated using a cryptographically secure random number generator.

Once a private key is generated, it must be protected against compromise. If an attacker can steal a user's private key using malware, phishing, or other methods, they have the ability to masquerade as that user on the distributed ledger, performing transactions on their behalf. Private keys that control accounts with access to elevated permissions on the distributed ledger or with large amounts of value stored within them should be in cold storage or stored on a device not accessible from the Internet.

Algorithmic Security

The other half of the security of public key cryptography is the security of the algorithm itself. This involves ensuring that the "hard" problem that the algorithm is built upon remains "hard."

If this is the case, then the only way to break the cryptography is via a brute-force search. If the private key is long enough to make this infeasible, then the protocol remains secure.

Attacking Public Key Cryptography

The security of public key cryptography boils down to the security of the private key and the difficulty of the mathematical problem that the algorithm uses for its asymmetry. If an attacker can compromise a private key or break this asymmetry, then public key cryptography becomes insecure.

Private Key Security

With public key cryptography, a user's private key is the only secret. The cryptographic algorithm and any parameters that it uses are public knowledge. This means that anyone with knowledge of a user's private key can decrypt messages and generate digital signatures while impersonating that user.

For this reason, private key security is essential to the security of asymmetric cryptography. Two of the primary ways in which this can go wrong are weak key generation and failure to properly protect the private key.

Weak Key Generation

Private keys are supposed to be random numbers that are generated to meet the requirements of the particular algorithm (key length, primacy, etc.). If a key is not random, then an attacker can potentially guess that key. This could allow them to generate transactions on a user's behalf, stealing cryptocurrency or interacting with smart contracts.

Weak Random Number Generation

Many blockchain users use a tool to generate private keys for their blockchain accounts. This functionality could be integrated into the software that they use to access the blockchain, or it could be a stand-alone website or service.

These tools should use a cryptographic random number generator (RNG) to create the users' private keys. However, some are implemented incorrectly or use a non-cryptographic RNG, leading to weak sources of randomness.

The story of the "Blockchain Bandit" demonstrates the risks of such an approach. A study by Independent Security Evaluators found that an attacker was scanning the Ethereum blockchain for account addresses generated using weak private keys.[1] As of January 13, 2018, the Blockchain Bandit had stolen 37,926 ETH from these accounts.

Another risk of using a third-party service for key generation is that the resulting private keys could be intentionally weak or recorded by the service to allow future theft. A 2019 study found that the source code for WalletGenerator.net deviated from the source code at the project's GitHub repository for some time after August 17, 2018.[2]

Testing the "bulk wallet" generator on the site found that attempts to create 1,000 keys resulted in different results for the non-malicious GitHub version and the malicious active version. The GitHub version properly generated 1,000 unique keys, while the active version only provided 120 unique keys per request. If these 1,000 keys were provided to different users, some would have the same key and access to one another's blockchain accounts.

Password-Based Private Keys

Brain wallet is a term for memorizing the private key associated with a blockchain account. While this has the benefit of being unhackable, most people struggle to remember a random series of letters and numbers.

One insecure solution to this problem is to generate a private key from an easily memorizable word or phrase. To do so, this seed phrase could be hashed with SHA-256 or another algorithm with the same length as the desired secret key.

BitMEX research did a study on this approach that they titled Call me Ishmael after a quote from *Moby Dick*.[3] The researchers generated secret keys using quotes from famous works such as *Moby Dick*, the Bitcoin white paper, and Jane Austen's books. Attackers guessed the passphrases for all of these accounts within a day, and one, "Call me Ishmael," only lasted 0.67 seconds.

Compromised Mnemonic Keys

For those wishing to memorize their blockchain private keys, mnemonic keys or seed phrases offer a more secure alternative to password-based keys. A mnemonic key is a set of 12 to 24 words pulled from a standard wordlist. Each word encodes 11 bits of randomness from the original key.

Mnemonic keys make private keys easier to memorize, but they also need to be properly protected, and even a partially compromised mnemonic key can leave a blockchain account open to attack. In 2020, Alistair Milne released 8 of 12 words of a mnemonic key one at a time, intending to release the last three or four at once to prevent brute-force attacks.[4] John Cantrell wrote a custom script that tried over 1 trillion possibilities in 30 hours to claim the 1 BTC in the account.[5]

Weak Key Security

After generating a private key, a blockchain user needs to preserve the secrecy of that key for the lifetime of the account. If an unauthorized party gains access to that key, they can generate transactions on the users' behalf and steal cryptocurrency from them.

Vulnerable Storage

Insecure storage of secret data has been a problem for far longer than blockchain has existed. Passwords written on sticky notes under a keyboard or saved in text documents on a computer have been a security challenge for decades.

With the introduction of blockchain technology, it should come as no surprise that private keys are regularly stored in locations where they can be easily stolen or lost forever. Countless blockchain accounts have been compromised by poor key management, and an estimated 30 percent of Bitcoin is lost forever due to lost private keys.[6]

Hardware wallets offer a potential solution by storing private keys on a device that uses a dedicated microprocessor to store keys and generate digital signatures so that the keys never leave the device. However, even hardware wallets can have security vulnerabilities. Dozens of vulnerabilities have been discovered in hardware wallets that can cause them to expose private keys or otherwise misbehave.[7]

Cryptocurrency Wallets and Exchanges

Many blockchain users don't want to manage their own private keys. Instead, they use a third-party service to store these keys. Common examples include cryptocurrency wallet services and exchanges.

With these wallets and exchanges, the security model for user accounts changes. Instead of having to guess a user's secret key, which should be a large random value, an attacker only needs to learn the user's password for the key management service and potentially defeat multifactor authentication (MFA).

This is a much easier problem for an attacker to solve. The following list includes some common approaches:

- **Password Guessing:** Many people have weak and reused passwords. This makes it trivial for an attacker to gain access to an account via brute-force password guessing or credential stuffing attacks.

- **Phishing:** Phishing attacks are a common way to steal passwords and MFA codes or deliver malware to target computers. In 2021, a phishing attack infected the computer of a bZx developer with malware that stole private keys, allowing tokens worth $55 million at the time to be stolen from the project and its users.[8]

- **SIM Swapping:** Many online services use SMS messages for MFA, so a SIM swapping attacker can gain access to these codes. In 2021, European law enforcement arrested eight individuals for involvement in a $100 million SIM swapping attack.[9]

- **Malware:** Some attacks on private keys are designed to replace legitimate software with malware that steals private keys or modifies transactions performed by the user. In April 2021, the EasyFi DeFi protocol lost over $46 million in tokens in a hack that used a malicious version of MetaMask to steal private keys.[10]

Malware

Blockchain technology is implemented as software. When users want to interact with a blockchain, they need to use their computers. This can mean typing private keys or mnemonic phrases into blockchain software for use in signing a transaction.

If a private key or mnemonic seed is entered into a computer, then it's potentially vulnerable to malware. Some malware, such as the Clippy Malware, is designed to scan the contents of the system clipboard or a computer's memory for data that resembles a private key or a blockchain address.

One such malware campaign was designed to redirect transactions performed by users of compromised machines. This malware monitored the clipboards of infected machines for data that matched any of 2.3 million Bitcoin addresses.[11] If it found a match, it would replace the address with the attacker's address. Unless the user double-checked the address after pasting, the transaction would be sent to the attacker rather than its intended recipient.

Algorithmic Security

While compromised private keys are the most common way for public key cryptography to be attacked, the algorithms themselves may also be insecure. However, no known attacks exist that could allow the asymmetric encryption algorithms used in blockchain to be broken on modern technology.

This is only true until large-scale quantum computing becomes available. Once this is the case, Shor's algorithm will force a transition to post-quantum encryption algorithms.

Shor's Algorithm

Many public key cryptography algorithms are based upon the "hard" problems of factoring the product of two large prime numbers or calculating a logarithm within a modulus. Using modern computers, the best way to solve these problems is through a brute-force search, which scales exponentially in difficulty with the length of the secret values used. Since the difficulty of legitimate operations only scales polynomially, it's possible to choose a key length that makes the system usable for a legitimate user but infeasible to attack.

Shor's algorithm is an algorithm written for quantum computers that solves these problems in a way that's more efficient than a brute-force search. With Shor's algorithm, the complexity of attacking classical public key cryptography changes from exponential to polynomial, just like the cost of legitimate operations.

This makes it impossible to use classical public key cryptography in a scheme that is secure against quantum computers. Even if the complexity of the "hard" operation grows several times faster than the "easy" one, an attacker can feasibly keep up by throwing more money at the problem. It doesn't matter if factoring is five times harder than multiplication if an eavesdropper has one hundred computers to your one.

Post-Quantum Cryptography

Shor's algorithm is a problem for classical asymmetric encryption algorithms because it breaks the asymmetry of the "hard" problems that these algorithms are based upon. If both multiplication and factoring have polynomial complexity, then it is infeasible to develop a system that is both usable and secure. Even if the complexity of factoring grows 100x faster than that of multiplication, an attacker can break it by spending 100x more than a legitimate user.

Hash Functions

Hash functions are at the core of blockchain technology. The main function of a hash function is to ensure the integrity of data. This is possible because hash functions are one-way, collision-resistant functions, meaning that it is infeasible to determine the input that produced a given output or find two inputs that produce the same output.

Providing the hash of a piece of data along with the data itself is a common way of ensuring the integrity of the data. File checksums use hash functions to ensure that the file has not been modified after creation (since finding another version of the data that produces the same hash is extremely unlikely). Computers store the hashed versions of passwords to maintain the confidentiality of the passwords since it's impossible to determine the original password from the hash and comparing the hash of a password to a stored hash is almost as secure as comparing the true passwords.

In blockchain (and other distributed ledger implementations), hash functions are commonly used to ensure the integrity of the data stored within the distributed ledger. Each block in a blockchain contains the hash of the previous block and a hash summarizing the transaction data stored within the block. As long as the hash function remains secure, the data in the distributed ledger cannot be modified without the modifications being detected.

Security Assumptions of Hash Functions

The security of hash functions is a major assumption of distributed ledger technology. Hash functions protect the integrity of the data stored within the distributed ledger and must have two important properties: preimage resistance and collision resistance.

Preimage Resistance

A preimage of a hash function is an input that produces a desired output. Hash functions must be preimage-resistant, meaning that, for a given output, it should be infeasible for someone to find an input that produces that output.

Preimage resistance is achieved by using a one-way function in a cryptographic hash function. One-way functions discard some information during their computations so that it is impossible to uniquely map an output to the input used to create it.

An example of a simple one-way function is the modulo operation, where the input is divided by the modulus and only the remainder of the division is retained. With an output of 5 modulo 10, the possible inputs are 5, 15, 25, and so on. Without additional knowledge, it is impossible to determine which of the possible inputs was used to create the output of 5.

Hash functions have an infinite space of potential inputs and a finite space of potential outputs because they can take any input and produce a fixed-size output. This means that hash functions map an infinite number of inputs to each potential output, making them inherently preimage-resistant.

Collision Resistance

The other important principle of hash functions for distributed ledger security is collision resistance. A hash function collision is when two inputs to the hash function can be found that produce the same output. There are two levels of collision resistance that a cryptographic hash function must have: weak collision resistance and strong collision resistance.

A hash function is weakly collision-resistant if, given an input m_1, it is difficult to find another input, m_2, that maps to the same output. Strong collision resistance means that it is difficult to find any pair of inputs that map to the same output. A cryptographic hash function used in distributed ledger technology needs to be both weakly and strongly collision-resistant.

THE PIGEONHOLE PRINCIPLE AND THE BIRTHDAY PARADOX

Hash functions are compressible functions, meaning they can take in an infinite number of inputs and produce a finite number of outputs. For example, the Keccak-256 hash function used in many distributed ledgers can take in any binary input and produces a 256-bit output.

According to the pigeonhole principle, this means that multiple inputs exist that produce the same output. Logically, if you have a function that produces 25 possible outputs and you have 26 possible inputs, at least 2 inputs must produce the same output. Every hash function must have collisions, but cryptographically secure hash functions make these collisions "difficult" to find.

A hash function is considered collision-resistant if the best way to find a solution is a brute-force search: trying randomly selected inputs and checking if the desired output is found. While 2^N inputs (where N is the length of the output in binary) must be tried to find a collision with certainty, according to the birthday paradox, a collision can be found with high probability after only $2^{N/2}$ attempts.

The birthday paradox describes the complexity of finding a collision within a set, such as the probability that two people in a room have the same birthday. While 356 people are necessary to guarantee a collision (ignoring leap days), only 23 are needed to have a 50 percent probability of a shared birthday. This is because the number of person-to-person pairings with 23 people is $(23*22)/2 = 253$. The probability that each has different birthdays is then $(364/365)^{253} = 0.4995$. Thus, the probability of a shared birthday is $1 - 0.4995 = 0.5005$. This paradox also applies to hash collisions, making an attacker's probability of success much higher than it seems like it should be.

Additional Security Requirements

While preimage resistance and collision resistance are the only requirements necessary for security, a hash function must have certain other properties to achieve these requirements. A cryptographic hash function must have a large state space and be a nonlocal function to protect it against successful brute-force attacks.

Large State Space

If a hash function is well-designed, the best way of finding a collision is searching through the set of possible inputs and looking for one that produces the desired output. In order to make this type of attack infeasible, the hash function needs to be designed so that it is unlikely that an attacker will successfully complete this search within a reasonable length of time.

The size of the space that needs to be searched to find a collision is determined by the size of the output of the hash function. By the pigeonhole principle, an attacker needs to test a set of inputs equal to the number of possible outputs in order to be certain of finding a collision. A strong cryptographic hash function will have a large enough output that attempting to search it using modern technology will take either too much time or too many resources to be feasible.

Several blockchains use the Keccak-256 hash function (a variant of the SHA-256 hash function). As its name suggests, this hash function has a 256-bit output, meaning that there are 2^{256} possible values of this output. For comparison, the known universe contains fewer than 2^{272} atoms,[12] so a hard drive made using all of these atoms would still be too small to store the complete set of options (modern hard drives use about 1 million atoms per bit[13]). While an attacker may get lucky and find a solution on their first try, the only way to be certain is to search the complete space of 2^{256} options.

Nonlocal Function

The other important property that a hash function needs for collision resistance is nonlocality. In a cryptographic hash function, two very similar inputs produce very dissimilar outputs. On average, hashing two inputs that differ by a single bit will produce outputs that differ in half of their bits.

The nonlocality of the hash function is important to collision resistance because it protects against hill-climbing attacks. In a hill-climbing attack, an attacker takes the following steps:

1. Select an input.
2. Hash the input.
3. Flip one bit of the input.
4. Hash the new input.
5. Compare the new input's hash with the current one's hash.

   a. If the new hash is closer to the target, retain the change and go to step 3.

   b. If the new hash is further from the target, discard the change and go to step 3.

A hill-climbing attack takes advantage of the locality of a function by making small changes and evaluating whether the change is positive or negative. By retaining positive changes and discarding negative ones, the attacker incrementally moves toward their goal (a collision).

Cryptographic hash functions are protected against this type of attack because it is impossible to evaluate whether a change is positive or negative. Since small changes to hash function inputs produce large, unpredictable changes to outputs, it's impossible to determine if the attacker is moving toward or away from an input that would produce a collision.

How the Blockchain Uses Hash Functions

The integrity protections offered by hash functions are crucial to blockchain technology. Three major places where hash functions appear on the blockchain are the blocks' "chains," their Merkle trees, and within digital signatures.

The Blocks' "Chains"

The blockchain gets its name from the fact that it is a set of blocks chained together. The "chains" in blockchain are hash functions.

Inside the header of each block in the blockchain is the hash of the previous block header. This both links the blockchain together, providing a clear ordering, and makes it more difficult to forge blocks.

Without these previous block hashes, modifying a past transaction in the distributed ledger would only require finding an alternative, valid version of the block that contains it. While the definition of a valid block depends on the consensus algorithm used by the blockchain, block creators regularly create new blocks, so it can't be too hard.

With the blocks' chains, the value of each block header depends on the previous one. A change to one block header changes the previous block hash in the next, which changes the previous block hash in the next, and so on.

These cascading changes mean that changing a single transaction in the blockchain requires finding an alternative version of both the block that contains it and every following block. Blockchain consensus algorithms are designed to make this much more difficult than faking a single block.

The only way to get around these cascading changes is if an attacker can find an alternative version of a block that doesn't change the previous block hash value in the next block. This is the definition of a hash collision: two hash inputs that produce the same output. If the blockchain is using a secure, collision-resistant hash function, this is infeasible.

Merkle Trees

The transactions contained within a block are stored in the block's body, not its header. This means that they are not included as an input to the hash function that implements the blocks' chains.

The immutability of blockchain transactions is protected by a Merkle tree. A Merkle tree is a binary tree whose internal nodes contain the hashes of their children.

An example of a Merkle tree is shown in Figure 2.1. The transactions contained within a block are shown at the bottom of the tree. Each leaf node of the tree contains the hash of the transaction below it, and all other nodes contain the hashes of their children's values concatenated together.

One of the major advantages of a Merkle tree is that it allows transaction data to be securely summarized by the root hash of the Merkle tree. Due to hash function collision resistance, it is infeasible to find two versions of the Merkle tree that produce the same root hash. By including just the root hash of the Merkle tree within the block header, a blockchain ensures that all transactions contained by it are protected from modification by the blocks' chains.

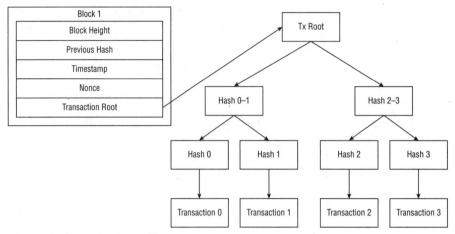

Figure 2.1: Example of a Merkle tree

Merkle trees also make it possible to prove that a transaction is contained within a Merkle tree or a given block without revealing any of the other transactions in that block. For example, proving the presence of Transaction 0 in the Merkle tree in Figure 2.1 to someone who has access to the block header only requires revealing the following values:

- Transaction 0
- Hash 1
- Hash 2-3

From the value of Transaction 0, it's possible to calculate Hash 0. By combining Hash 0 and Hash 1, the user could calculate Hash 0-1. With Hash 0-1 and Hash 2-3, the user can calculate the value of Tx Root and compare it to the value of Tx Root in the block header.

These proofs are commonly used by Simplified Payment Verification (SPV) nodes to verify the inclusion of a transaction within a block without downloading the entire block body. These SPV nodes track the block headers and their connecting chains but verify transactions by requesting these proofs.

Digital Signatures

The discussion of digital signatures in the context of public key cryptography left out one crucial component. The data actually "encrypted" by the private key and "decrypted" by the public key is the hash of the message, not the message itself.

The use of hash functions helps to shrink the size of the digital signature by securely compressing it into a fixed-size value. Due to the hash function collision resistance, it is infeasible to find another message that would produce the same hash output and not invalidate the digital signature. As a result, hashing the message and comparing hashes is nearly as secure as comparing the messages themselves.

Attacking Hash Functions

If a hash function is secure and collision-resistant, the only means of finding a hash collision is via a brute-force attack. With quantum computing, Grover's algorithm makes this attack easier to perform; however, it doesn't break hash function security.

Brute Force

Hash functions are designed to be collision-resistant, meaning that it is infeasible to find two inputs to the hash function that produce the same output. However, the pigeonhole principle states that it's possible to break collision resistance if you try hard enough.

A brute-force attack on a secure hash function is infeasible as long as the hash function has no exploitable vulnerabilities. A well-designed hash function that is a one-way, nonlocal function with a large state space is infeasible to attack.

The Lisk blockchain provides an example of what can happen if a hash function does not fulfill all of these properties. In Lisk, account addresses were calculated by hashing a public key and truncating the result to a 64-byte address.[14]

With only 2^{64} potential addresses, a brute-force attack against this blockchain is entirely possible. At the time of writing, the Bitcoin network had a hash rate of over 2^{67} hashes per second, meaning that it could find multiple potential private keys for each address every second.

Lisk only tied a public key to an address when it created a transaction or voted for a delegate. This meant that accounts containing cryptocurrency could have that cryptocurrency extracted by the first person to find a valid private key for it. One of these vulnerable accounts contained over $48 million at the time of the vulnerability's discovery.

This vulnerability was discovered by an ethical hacker and reported to the Lisk developers, who issued a warning to users to generate a transaction that secured their accounts. However, due to the nature of the vulnerability, it's impossible to determine if the user who did so for an account was the legitimate owner of any cryptocurrency that it contained.

Grover's Algorithm

Like Shor's algorithm, Grover's algorithm is designed to run on a quantum computer that threatens the security of distributed ledgers using classical cryptography. Unlike Shor's algorithm, Grover's algorithm threatens the security of modern hash functions but does not completely break them the way that Shor's algorithm breaks classical public key cryptography.

On classical computers, the most efficient way to find a collision for a secure hash function is to search through a set of possible inputs equal to the size of the space of possible outputs. Hash functions are designed to make this infeasible by making the space of possible outputs too large to search efficiently.

Grover's algorithm makes the process of finding collisions more efficient for an attacker. On a classical computer, searching for a collision to a hash function with an N-bit output requires 2^N evaluations of the hash function. With Grover's algorithm and a quantum computer, this drops to `sqrt(2`^{N}`)` or $2^{N/2}$ evaluations.

However, Grover's algorithm does not completely break the security of classical hash functions since the desired level of security can be achieved by doubling the size of the output. SHA-256 is theoretically as equally secure against a quantum computer as SHA-128 is against a classical one. As quantum computers become more common, new hash functions will need to be developed with output lengths sufficient to protect against attacks using Grover's algorithm.

Threat Modeling for Cryptographic Algorithms

Attacks against the public key cryptography and hash functions used in blockchain technology can have impacts on several areas of the STRIDE threat model:

- **Spoofing:** Compromised private keys enable an attacker to masquerade as a user and generate blockchain transactions on their behalf.

- **Tampering:** A hash function collision in the blocks' chains, a Merkle tree, or digital signature can break the immutability of the distributed ledger.

- **Information Disclosure:** A compromised private key could allow decryption of messages intended for the owner of a blockchain account.

- **Elevation of Privileges:** A compromised private key provides unauthorized access to a user's blockchain account.

Data Structures

The primary function of the blockchain is data storage. The blockchain network cooperates to maintain a distributed, immutable digital ledger that tracks the history of the blockchain network.

Under the hood, a blockchain may use a variety of different data structures to store information about the state of the network. However, the two most important data structures in blockchain are the transaction and the block.

Transactions

The transaction is the basic unit of data on the blockchain's digital ledger. When a blockchain user wants to transfer value or interact with a smart contract, they create a transaction and broadcast it to the blockchain network.

What's In a Transaction?

Different blockchains may have slightly different transaction formats; however, many of the core fields are the same. In Bitcoin, a transaction contains the following seven fields:

- **Version:** The version of the transaction.
- **Witness Marker:** Indicates that the transaction uses Segregated Witness.
- **Flags:** Flags are used for parsing if the witness marker is present.
- **Inputs:** An array of inputs to the transaction.
- **Outputs:** An array of outputs from the transaction.
- **Witnesses:** An array of witnesses for the transaction.
- **Lock Time:** The time for a time-locked transaction to remain locked.

As shown, a Bitcoin transaction can include multiple different transfers of value. If Segregated Witness is used, each input has its own corresponding witness, which contains the digital signature that authorizes the use of that input within the transaction.

Unlike Bitcoin, Ethereum specifies a single intended recipient for a transaction, which is either an external address (i.e., a user account) or a smart contract address. Similar to Bitcoin, smart contracts can perform multiple actions within a single transaction, which are called *internal transactions*.

Inside the Life Cycle of a Transaction

Transactions are not immediately added to the blockchain's immutable digital ledger. Transactions are added to the blockchain as part of blocks, and several stages occur between their creation and inclusion in the ledger.

After being created, a transaction is broadcast to other nodes via the blockchain's peer-to-peer network. Each node stores pending transactions in a mempool for inclusion in later blocks.

When it is time to create a new block, a block producer draws from this pool of available transactions. Before including a transaction in a potential block, the creator checks it to ensure that it is valid and that it doesn't conflict with any other transactions currently on the blockchain (a *double spend*).

After a valid block is produced, the block creator transmits it to the rest of the blockchain network via the peer-to-peer network. Each of these nodes also validates the transactions within a block and, if they are valid, accepts the block. This involves adding the block to the digital ledger and performing state updates, such as determining the new allocation of cryptocurrency within the blockchain network or executing code on a smart contract platform.

Attacking Transactions

Transactions are the basic building blocks of the blockchain and lie completely under the control of a blockchain user. Malicious transactions can be used in various attacks to exploit vulnerable blockchain nodes and other systems.

Malformed or Invalid Transactions

As part of the process of creating blocks and updating the ledger, blockchain nodes must read and validate the contents of every transaction. This ensures that double-spend attacks and other invalid transactions are not included on the blockchain.

Blockchain transactions are untrusted user input and may be intentionally malformed to exploit vulnerable nodes. If a vulnerable node processes an invalid transaction, it may crash or exhibit other undesirable behavior.

Countermeasures

Exploitation of blockchain software with malformed transactions requires a vulnerability to exploit. Secure code development practices and code reviews are the best protection against this threat.

Case Study

Blockchain software is software, and all software has bugs. As a result, multiple vulnerabilities have been discovered in blockchain transaction validation code that have been or could have been exploited over the years.

One significant example was the 2010 Bitcoin hack, which created over 184 billion Bitcoin out of nothing.[15] This attack was enabled by an integer overflow vulnerability in the Bitcoin Core software. A malicious transaction performed two transfers that, when summed with some other values, overflowed to 50.51, which passed the transaction validation check.

However, the actual transfers were performed separately, which did not trigger the overflow and allowed a massive amount of Bitcoin to be transferred to the attacker's account. This vulnerability was fixed soon afterward with a hard fork that patched the vulnerability and rolled back history to the block right before the attack.

Transaction Malleability

In the Bitcoin blockchain, transactions are uniquely identified by a transaction ID (txid). This txid is calculated by double-hashing the contents of a transaction.

Transaction malleability attacks took advantage of the fact that the unlocking script for a transaction is included in the hash, and the format of the script was not always properly validated. This could allow an attacker to modify the unlock script of a pending transaction without invalidating it.

This modification would change the txid of that transaction. If the sender of the transaction only uses the txid to identify transactions on the blockchain, the recipient could use transaction malleability to claim that they never received a payment. This could cause the sender to repeat the transaction, paying the recipient twice.

Countermeasures

Bitcoin addressed transaction malleability issues with Segregated Witness (SegWit), which moves witnesses out of transaction inputs. Since these digital signatures are no longer included in the txid calculation, this fixes the transaction malleability problem.

Other blockchains have addressed the malleability issue through different means. For example, Bitcoin Cash (BCH) split from the Bitcoin network over a disagreement over SegWit. Instead, BCH has addressed various sources of transaction malleability in a series of independent upgrades.[16]

Case Study

Mt. Gox was a cryptocurrency exchange that went bankrupt. Before announcing bankruptcy, the exchange blamed frozen Bitcoin withdrawals on a repeated transaction malleability attack. By exploiting the transaction malleability bug and claiming that they had never received withdrawal transactions, attackers were able to extract 386 Bitcoin (worth $203,000) from the exchange.[17]

Serialization Vulnerabilities

Serialization is a technique for converting an object or a collection of variables into a single series of bits for transmission or storage. If the structure of the object is well-defined, then the recipient of the data can deserialize it into the original object or set of variables.

Blockchain nodes commonly serialize and deserialize untrusted user input, including transactions, blocks, and other data structures. This creates the potential for serialization vulnerabilities where deserialization code makes assumptions about the data that it receives and processes it without verifying these assumptions first.

Serialization vulnerabilities can result in integer and buffer overflow vulnerabilities, infinite loops or recursion, or other issues. Exploitation of these vulnerabilities can allow an attacker to execute malicious code or perform a denial-of-service (DoS) attack against vulnerable software.

Countermeasures

Serialization vulnerabilities are the result of failing to perform proper input validation on untrusted data before deserializing it. Verifying that serialized data follows the protocol and is valid before deserializing or processing it can protect against these vulnerabilities.

Case Study

In 2018, a serialization vulnerability was discovered in the NEO smart contract platform that could have enabled a denial-of-service (DoS) attack against the network.[18] The software's StackItem type can contain different types of data, including arrays, whose size and child elements would be serialized as well.

The security researchers who discovered this vulnerability found that an array, *a*, could be added as an element of itself. Attempting to deserialize this would result in an infinite loop, causing a NEO node attempting to process the data to crash with a StackOverflowException.

Block Explorer Injection

Block explorers are websites that are designed to provide visibility into what is happening on the blockchain. Block explorers allow inspection of each block on the blockchain down to the contents of individual transaction inputs and outputs.

Blockchain transactions have a defined structure, but they also have room for arbitrary data. For example, the Bitcoin genesis block is famous for containing a quote from the UK newspaper *The Times*, "*The Times* 03/Jan/2009 Chancellor on brink of second bailout for banks."[19]

With the ability to embed arbitrary data within a transaction, it is possible that an attacker could craft a transaction designed to exploit vulnerable block explorers or other software that processes transactions.

For example, a blockchain transaction could be designed to contain a cross-site scripting (XSS) exploit. If a vulnerable block explorer displays the malicious transaction, then it could expose visitors to an XSS attack.

Countermeasures

Injection attacks are a common attack vector for web applications, and this threat is only different due to the potential sources of the malicious user data. Performing input validation and implementing standard protections against XSS and other web application attacks can help to protect against this threat.

Case Study

EtherDelta is a decentralized exchange that included a frontend application that showed information about the tokens that users could trade. As a frontend for a trading platform, it also had users enter their private keys to perform transactions.

This frontend application contained an XSS vulnerability that could be exploited via malicious token contracts.[20] The vulnerable page extracted the name of a token from the contract code and embedded it within the web page. An attacker exploited this by creating a malicious contract whose name included JavaScript code that was designed to access the private keys entered by the user and send them to the attacker.

The attacker posted links to their contract on Discord and Slack. By stealing private keys from visitors to the site, the attacker was able to steal thousands of dollars from their compromised accounts.

Blocks

Transactions are added to the blockchain's distributed ledger as parts of blocks. The blocks are created by block producers selected via the blockchain consensus algorithm.

Inside a Block

As mentioned previously, a blockchain block is made up of two parts. The block header is a fixed-size structure that contains metadata about the block and is the value covered by the previous block hash. While the contents of a block header can vary from one blockchain to another, a Bitcoin block header includes the following fields:

- Version
- Previous block hash
- Merkle root
- Time stamp
- Difficulty target
- Nonce

Blocks add transactions to the distributed ledger, but these aren't included in the block header. The other part of the block is the block body, which contains these transactions.

Transactions in the body of a block are organized in the same order that they appear in the block's Merkle tree. This enables anyone with access to the entire block to recompute the Merkle tree and compare its root value to the one stored within the block header. If they match, then the transactions in the block have presumably not been modified since the block was created.

Attacking Blockchain Blocks

Like transactions, blockchain blocks contain untrusted data and are processed by every node within the network as part of the ledger update process. While potential vulnerabilities in the block creation process are covered in a later chapter, note that the block data structure can be used in different attacks.

Serialization Vulnerabilities

The potential for serialization vulnerabilities was mentioned in the discussion of attacks against transactions because they can contain serialized data. Similarly, block headers are serialized for transmission on the blockchain, potentially enabling a malformed block header to exploit vulnerable nodes.

Bitcoin Leaf-Node Weakness

Merkle trees are binary trees that summarize the transactions within a block in the transaction root. The number of layers within a Merkle tree depends on the number of transactions the block contains.

The Bitcoin Leaf-Node weakness took advantage of the fact that Bitcoin doesn't specify the depth of a Merkle tree. An attacker could theoretically construct a transaction that appears to be an inner node of a Merkle tree, which summarizes two transactions within a 64-byte hash.[21]

With a 72-bit brute-force attack, an attacker could craft a pair of transactions that would hash to this 64-byte hash. The attacker could then generate a valid proof to an SPV node that these child transactions were included in the blockchain when they were not.

Countermeasures

Version 0.14 of the Bitcoin blockchain addressed this issue by disallowing any transactions that were exactly 64 bytes in length. Additionally, transactions valuable enough to make such an attack profitable would use a full node for verification, which does not rely on an SPV proof.

Threat Modeling for Data Structures

The transactions and blocks used to organize data in the blockchain are under an attacker's control. This allows them to be used in attacks against most areas of the STRIDE threat model:

- **Spoofing:** Exploitation of injection vulnerabilities in block explorers and other frontend systems can result in the compromise of private keys. These can be used to masquerade as the user and perform transactions on their behalf.

- **Tampering:** Transaction malleability can allow an attacker to change the hash and transaction ID of unconfirmed transactions, changing how they are recorded on the blockchain.

- **Denial of Service:** Malformed transactions or blocks can be used to crash vulnerable nodes.

- **Elevation of Privileges:** Theft of private keys through block explorer injection attacks can grant unauthorized access to user accounts.

Conclusion

This chapter explored the security of the fundamentals of the blockchain ecosystem. The public key cryptography, hash functions, transactions, and blocks are the core components used to build blockchain's decentralized, immutable ledger.

In the next chapter, we'll step up a level to look at the protocols used to achieve consensus in the blockchain and to define how blocks are created and added to the digital ledger. These protocols use the cryptographic algorithms and data structures explored here to provide the vital functionality and security guarantees of the blockchain.

Notes

1. www.ise.io/casestudies/ethercombing

2. https://medium.com/mycrypto/disclosure-key-generation-vulnerability-found-on-walletgenerator-net-potentially-malicious-3d8936485961

3. https://blog.bitmex.com/call-me-ishmael

4. https://twitter.com/alistairmilne/status/1266037520715915267

5. https://medium.com/@johncantrell97/how-i-checked-over-1-trillion-mnemonics-in-30-hours-to-win-a-bitcoin-635fe051a752

6. https://blog.chainalysis.com/reports/money-supply

7. https://thecharlatan.ch/List-Of-Hardware-Wallet-Hacks

8. https://therecord.media/hacker-steals-55-million-from-bzx-defi-platform

9. www.europol.europa.eu/media-press/newsroom/news/ten-hackers-arrested-for-string-of-sim-swapping-attacks-against-celebrities

10. https://medium.com/easify-network/easyfi-security-incident-pre-post-mortem-33f2942016e9

11. www.bleepingcomputer.com/news/security/clipboard-hijacker-malware-monitors-23-million-bitcoin-addresses

12. www.universetoday.com/36302/atoms-in-the-universe

13. www.bbc.com/news/technology-16543497

14. https://research.kudelskisecurity.com/2018/01/16/blockchains-how-to-steal-millions-in-264-operations

15. https://news.bitcoin.com/bitcoin-history-part-10-the-184-billion-btc-bug

16. https://bitcoincashresearch.org/t/transaction-malleability-malfix-segwit-sighash-noinput-sighash-spendanyoutput-etc/279

17. www.coindesk.com/markets/2014/03/27/study-mt-gox-may-have-lost-just-386-btc-due-to-transaction-malleability

18. https://blog.360totalsecurity.com/en/alert-dos-vulnerability-is-discovered-to-crash-the-entire-neo-network

19. https://en.bitcoin.it/wiki/Genesis_block

20. https://medium.com/hackernoon/how-one-hacker-stole-thousands-of-dollars-worth-of-cryptocurrency-with-a-classic-code-injection-a3aba5d2bff0

21. https://bitslog.com/2018/06/09/leaf-node-weakness-in-bitcoin-merkle-tree-design

CHAPTER

3

Protocols

Blockchains are protocols, not specific implementations. Like HTTP, which defines how web servers and browsers should communicate, blockchain protocols define how nodes should work together to maintain the decentralized digital ledger.

Blockchain protocols are designed to incentivize the nodes in the blockchain network to work in its best interests while assuming that a certain percentage of nodes are greedy and potentially malicious. Blockchain protocols are designed to make it more profitable to play by the rules than to cheat.

The blockchain's ledger is regularly updated with the addition of new blocks. The two main protocols that enable new blocks define how the network should choose who creates the next one (consensus) and how that selected block creator should go about doing so.

Consensus

Distributed ledgers are designed to operate as distributed, decentralized systems. Each node in the network stores its own copy of the distributed ledger and is responsible for keeping that copy in sync with the rest of the network.

In blockchain-based systems, this is accomplished using consensus algorithms. These algorithms formalize the process by which the creator of the next block in the blockchain is selected. In the following sections, I discuss how some of the major consensus algorithms work, their security assumptions, and some common attacks against them.

Key Concepts in Blockchain Consensus

Blockchain consensus algorithms are designed to implement decentralized decision making. Each node in the network needs to be able to independently determine who the creator of the next block should be and come up with the same answer as everyone else.

While making these decisions, blockchain nodes need to account for a few potential problems. Malicious nodes in the network may attempt to mislead other nodes for their own gain. Simple majority vote is not a workable approach to making decisions. The network may not achieve consensus, leading to multiple versions of the blockchain.

One of the major contributions of Satoshi Nakamoto in the Bitcoin white paper was developing solutions for these problems that work for a blockchain network. These approaches support decentralized decision making and scale to networks the size of Bitcoin.

Byzantine Generals Problem

The Byzantine Generals Problem (BGP) is a computer science problem designed by Leslie Lamport.[1] It describes the problem of distributed decision making in an environment where some decision-makers and communication paths cannot be trusted.

In BGP, multiple armies are laying siege to a city and need to decide on what to do next. The majority of the generals either need to agree to attack all at once or retreat all at once. If the group does not reach consensus, they will be defeated by the defenders of the city. Since the armies are spread around the city and the generals cannot leave their armies, they need to communicate via messenger.

The situation is complicated by the fact that some of the generals can be traitors, sending false messages or failing to send messages at all. To achieve consensus, the king sends a message to every general with his orders, and every general relays this message to every other general. As a result, every general receives multiple messages stating the king's wishes. Since some generals may be malicious, these messages may be contradictory. However, as long as two-thirds of the generals are good, it is possible to achieve consensus.

Solutions to the Byzantine Generals Problem have existed for some time now, but they were too inefficient for large-scale use. In order to operate, blockchains need to solve the Byzantine Generals Problem since they are also a distributed system trying to come to an agreement (the contents of the next block) while dealing with potential traitors (malicious nodes). Blockchain consensus algorithms are designed to provide a scalable solution to BGP and are called Byzantine Fault Tolerant (BFT) if they manage to do so.

Security via Scarcity

The simplest approach to decentralized decision making is majority vote. However, a straightforward majority vote doesn't work for blockchain due to the potential for a Sybil attack.

Blockchain systems are designed to be anonymous, and anyone can create a blockchain account. In a Sybil attack, a malicious user creates many fake accounts, which only requires generating a private key for a new address on the blockchain. If a blockchain implemented consensus via majority vote, a Sybil attacker has a disproportionate vote and potentially could control the majority of accounts.

The name *Sybil attack* is inspired by a book titled *Sybil*, which is about a woman with dissociative identity disorder. However, the subject of the book later admitted that the multiple identities were fake, just like an attacker's multiple accounts on the blockchain.

Instead of providing each account with equal control over the state of the ledger, blockchain consensus algorithms use a scarce resource to represent control over the blockchain. While different consensus algorithms use different scarce resources and apply them in different ways, a user's control over the block creation process is proportional to the percentage of the scarce resource they control. Since the block creator decides what is and isn't included in the ledger, this control over the scarce resource equates to control over the blockchain's ledger and its history.

The relationship between a resource's supply, demand, and price is a core principle of economics. If an item's demand increases relative to the supply, the price increases as well. An attacker attempting to accumulate enough of the finite resource to gain control of a blockchain's ledger increases the demand for a resource with a fixed supply. As the demand increases and the available supply shrinks (as the attacker accumulates all that is for sale), the price continues to rise.

In a decentralized system, there is no authority that can punish misbehavior, so users must want to behave in order for the system to work. Blockchain attempts to incentivize participation in the block creation process and stimulates demand for the scarce resource by paying nodes to create blocks. At the same time, it tries to prevent any one user from accumulating too much power by making such an attack too expensive to be feasible or profitable.

The Longest Chain Rule

A valid version of the blockchain is one whose blocks contain only valid transactions and that follows the rules of the blockchain consensus algorithm. For many consensus algorithms, this means that it is possible to have multiple valid versions of the same block and multiple divergent blockchains.

Blockchain systems lack a centralized authority that can decide which of two versions of the blockchain's distributed ledger is the "correct" one. Blockchains require a way to do so in a decentralized fashion, so they use the longest chain rule.

Under the longest chain rule, the "longer" of two conflicting blockchains is the one that a node should accept. In this context, *longer* means the version that required more work to create. For some consensus algorithms, this is literally the one with a greater number of blocks, but in others, a short chain of difficult-to-create blocks may beat out a longer one of easier blocks.

The longest chain rule implements the principle of majority vote using the scarce resources mentioned previously. Whichever version of the blockchain is longer should be the one supported by the majority of the scarce resource. The percentage of the scarce resource that a node or group controls is proportional to the probability of being selected to create a block. If more blocks are created by the supporters of one chain than by the creators of the other, then that chain should logically control more of the scarce resource.

Under the longest chain rule, a node may be forced to replace its previously accepted version of the blockchain with a new one. This is why blockchain transactions are said to only offer probabilistic finalization. While any block can theoretically be replaced by a different version, this becomes more difficult as more blocks are built on top of it. The blocks' chains and blockchain consensus algorithms are designed to make major reorganizations of the blockchain difficult to the point of being impossible.

Proof of Work

Proof of Work is the oldest blockchain consensus algorithm. Satoshi Nakamoto described it in 2008 in the Bitcoin white paper, which introduced the concept of blockchain to the world.

Proof of Work uses computational power as its scarce resource. The more calculations that a miner can perform, the higher probability of finding a valid block that the rest of the network will accept.

Introduction to Proof of Work

Blocks in a Proof of Work blockchain have two parts: the header and the body. The body contains the transaction data stored in the block, while the header contains four important fields:

- **Timestamp:** When the block was created
- **Transaction Hash:** Root hash of the Merkle tree containing the transactions in the block
- **Previous Block Hash:** Hash of previous block, chaining them together
- **Nonce:** A random value generated by the block creator

The Proof of Work consensus algorithm is designed to make it difficult to create a valid block but easy to validate one. In Proof of Work, a valid block is one whose header hashes to a value less than a certain threshold. Often, this threshold is referred to as the hash of the header having a certain number of leading zeros.

The properties of hash functions make the Proof of Work algorithm both possible and secure. Hash function nonlocality means that similar inputs produce very dissimilar outputs. By modifying the value of the nonce in the block header, Proof of Work miners can create headers with very different hashes that potentially fulfill the requirement that this value be less than the threshold.

Hash function preimage resistance means that the hash of a given block header is unpredictable. As a result, the only method of finding a valid block is by trying different nonce values until a miner hits upon a usable one. This is where the scarce resource of computational power comes into play. The greater the amount of computing power that a miner controls, the more hash calculations they can perform and the higher the probability that they are the one who finds a valid version of the current block.

Difficulty Targets in Proof of Work

The threshold used to determine whether or not a block is valid is based on the current difficulty target. This difficulty target can change over time as the total hash rate of the blockchain network grows or shrinks. The goal is to set the difficulty target so that the network is able to create a new valid block at a set rate.

For example, Bitcoin's target block rate is 10 minutes. This means that, on average, a block is created every 10 minutes. Due to the unpredictability of the mining process, some blocks are created more quickly and some take longer. However, the difficulty target is set so that the average number of potential nonces that it takes to find a valid block can be tested within 10 minutes at the blockchain's current hash rate.

Difficulty targets are adjusted at regular intervals in a decentralized fashion. All users in the blockchain network can see the times that each block was created and determine the actual block creation rate. At predefined intervals, they will multiply the current difficulty target by the ratio of the actual and target block times to create a new target that reflects the current resources of the blockchain network.

Security of Proof of Work

While many different types of attacks can be performed against a Proof of Work blockchain, three are designed specifically to attack the Proof of Work consensus algorithm. A 51% attack is a "brute-force" approach to taking over the network, while selfish and SPV mining are designed to allow an attacker to take over without committing the same number of resources as in a 51% attack.

An attacker can also take advantage of the mechanics of Proof of Work to disrupt the operation of the blockchain. One method is by forcing artificial difficulty updates for Proof of Work consensus.

51% Attack

The 51% attack is probably the most well-known attack against a blockchain and is described in the Bitcoin white paper. Proof of Work is designed to enforce consensus based upon majority vote where the "votes" are the hash calculations performed by miners during the block creation process.

If an attacker has a majority of the network's hash power (i.e., 51%), they are likely to win the race to create every new block and have control over the blockchain. While it's possible that the rest of the network could beat the attacker to creating one or more blocks, it is statistically unlikely that they will be able to maintain this lead. If the attacker can create and maintain the longest version of the blockchain, users following the blockchain protocol are obliged to accept it over the shorter option.

Countermeasures

A 51% attack is extremely difficult to prevent if an attacker has the resources to perform it. In fact, it has been said that it's impossible to have a truly decentralized system without being vulnerable to a 51% attack. Two approaches that have been tried are checkpointing and fining miners who attempt to perform one.

Checkpointing   In a blockchain using checkpointing, miners occasionally checkpoint a block on the chain and refuse to accept a version of the blockchain with a different version of that block, even if the other blockchain version is longer. The issue with this approach is that it risks either dividing the network or centralization.

If each user individually checkpoints blocks, there is the possibility that users will checkpoint different versions of the same block. As a result, these nodes will refuse to accept each other's version of the ledger, making it impossible for the network to be reunited.

If a single user generates checkpoints and distributes them (to avoid network fragmentation), then the blockchain system has become centralized. Neither of these options is good for blockchain security, so checkpointing is rarely used.

Fining   Another option for preventing 51% is fining miners who are performing a 51% attack. In general, 51% attacks are intended to facilitate double-spends, where an attacker publishes one version of a transaction, waits for it to be accepted, and then publishes a longer version of the blockchain that includes a contradictory version of the transaction. Since the longer version will be accepted and only one version of the transaction can be accepted, the original transaction is ignored.

In order to successfully perform a double-spend attack, the attacker must build the contradictory version of the blockchain in secret and not reveal it until the original transaction is accepted, which is typically after three blocks have been built on top of the block containing the transaction. This means that the early blocks in this divergent chain are only visible to the network long after they were created. On Bitcoin, the earliest block on the divergent chain would be published over half an hour after its creation time, which is significantly longer than can be explained by network delays.

One option is to fine miners who created blocks that are first seen by the network long after their creation time. This disincentivizes a 51% attack by making the miner lose money creating malicious blocks instead of being rewarded.

The issue with this approach is that delays in block creations can also happen for legitimate reasons. Later, we'll talk about denial-of-service attacks where an attacker can cause the rate at which blocks are created to slow. If blocks cannot be created before the cutoff that incurs a penalty, the blockchain may cease to function, as legitimate miners will not create blocks for fear of being penalized.

Case Studies

The cost of performing a 51% attack depends on the amount of computing power devoted to performing Proof of Work calculations on the blockchain. The greater the hash rate, the more expensive and less likely a 51% attack.

Over a dozen smaller blockchains have experienced a 51% attack, including well-known ones such as Ethereum Classic (ETC) and Bitcoin Satoshi's Vision (BSV).[2] These cryptocurrencies have a relatively low hash rate, making 51% attacks using rented cloud-based hashing infrastructure possible.

The Verge cryptocurrency was the victim of a 51% attack in which the attacker took advantage of the design of the protocol to perform the attack with approximately 10 percent of the blockchain's hash rate.[3] This attack exploited the design of the blockchain's protocol to drive down the difficulty threshold on one of its five mining algorithms.

As a result, miners using the Scrypt algorithm could find blocks much more easily than those using the other four algorithms. Assuming an even distribution of hash power across the five algorithms, this meant that 20 percent of the hash power was guaranteed to find every block. This allowed the attacker to create blocks faster than everyone else simply by controlling 10 percent of the overall hash rate and beating out other Scrypt miners.

SPV Mining

SPV mining takes advantage of the existence of Simplified Payment Verification (SPV) node software. When a new block is created, an SPV node will download only the header of the block for verification. It ignores the Merkle tree containing transaction data unless it needs to verify a particular transaction within a block. These nodes are not intended for use in mining but only for taking advantage of the services provided by the blockchain system.

SPV miners take advantage of the rules of the blockchain protocol to give themselves a head start at mining. When a traditional miner receives a new block, they take the following steps:

1. Download and verify the block header.
2. Download and validate transaction data.

3. Update pool of pending transactions.

4. Build a new block using valid transactions.

5. Begin mining the new block.

The steps of downloading and validating transactions can be time-consuming but are necessary. It's possible that a malicious user has created two contradictory transactions and transmitted them to the network. If one has already been added to the ledger, the other cannot be included as well. Before building a block, a miner needs to ensure that both the previous block and their current block contain only legitimate transactions. If not, they are wasting their time and resources mining the block as no legitimate user will accept it.

SPV miners skip steps 2 and 3 in the mining process in order to give themselves a head start. They do so by mining a block that contains only a single transaction: the one paying them the set reward for creating a block. This block is perfectly valid and has no chance of including invalid transactions, allowing them to start mining as soon as they have the hash of the previous block.

Countermeasures

SPV mining relies on the fact that it takes some time to perform verification of transactions in the previous and current blocks. The Bitcoin network has had some success in reducing SPV mining attacks by increasing the efficiency of these operations for their clients.

An SPV miner is making a trade-off between the increase in block rewards gained by mining more blocks (due to their head starts) and the loss of transaction fees due to mining empty blocks. Increasing the efficiency of verification code and the fact that block rewards decrease over time in most cryptocurrency blockchains will quickly make SPV mining an unprofitable form of attack.

Case Study

In 2018, the Etherdig Ethereum mining pool performed extensive SPV mining.[4] In three months, the pool created 1,250 blocks that did not validate a single transaction. This attack netted the pool 3,750 ETH worth $862,500 at the time.

Selfish Mining

A 51% attack requires significant resources on the part of the attacker, which may be infeasible to acquire. Selfish mining allows an attacker to perform a 51% attack with less than half of the network's total hash rate. It also can be used by malicious miners to increase their probability of creating a new block.

In a Proof of Work blockchain, the block rate is just a target. The difficulty is set so that it takes that amount of time to find a solution to the Proof of Work puzzle on average; however, a solution could also be found on the first try or require much longer than the target.

A selfish miner uses this knowledge to gain an advantage in block creation. If they have found a valid block for the current round, it is unlikely that another one will be found soon. Creation of a new block in the blockchain requires knowledge of the previous block since its hash is included in the new block's header. At the moment of block creation, only the creator of the block has this knowledge and is able to start mining the next block.

A selfish miner will deliberately conceal their knowledge of a valid version of the current block in order to gain a head start in creating the next block in the chain. This head start allows them to try some potential nonce values before any other node can begin mining that block.

With this head start, an attacker with only 49 percent of the network's hash rate may be capable of launching a 51% attack. For miners without this much hash rate, selfish mining still provides an increase in their probability of finding the next block, which increases their chances of earning block rewards.

Countermeasures

Unfortunately, it's difficult to protect against selfish mining. These attackers take advantage of the longest chain rule and the difficulty of Proof of Work mining to game the system and earn increased rewards.

Case Study

In 2018, the Ethereum mining pool F2Pool potentially performed a selfish mining attack.[5] This pool controlled 12.5 percent of the blockchain's hash rate and combined selfish and SPV mining techniques. F2Pool created an alternative version of the blockchain faster than the rest of the network, taking advantage of the fact that empty blocks could be created about 15 percent faster than legitimate ones.

When the pool's blockchain surpassed the legitimate one in length, it published it, causing other nodes to accept it under the longest chain rule. While this attack was not used to perform double-spends, it did net the pool additional block rewards.

Denial of Service: Artificial Difficulty Increases

Proof of Work blockchains attempt to tune the difficulty of finding a valid block to the network's hash rate. As hash rate rises and falls, the difficulty target changes as well to keep the block rate near the target.

This provides an opportunity for an attacker to perform a Denial-of-Service (DoS) attack to degrade the blockchain's ability to create new blocks. By adding more hash power to the blockchain network, the attacker can drive up the difficulty target at the next update because the network perceives that it is creating blocks too quickly.

If the attacker then removes this extra computational power from the blockchain, then the difficulty target is set too high for the remaining nodes. As a result, blocks will be created more slowly until the next time the network updates its difficulty threshold. In the case of the Bitcoin network, updates are performed every 2,016 blocks, which is two weeks at a 10-minute block interval. With a slower block rate, this update will take even longer to perform, extending the impacts of the DoS attack.

Another variant on this attack involves performing a DoS attack against legitimate miners via malware, Distributed DoS (DDoS), and so on. This has the same effect of dropping the hash rate, slowing block production.

Countermeasures

Proof of Work blockchains' difficulty targets are designed to rise and fall as the hash rate changes. Also, it can be difficult to differentiate between an artificial difficulty increase and one caused by benign miners leaving the network.

Proof of Stake

After Proof of Work (PoW), Proof of Stake is probably the most famous blockchain consensus algorithm. It consumes much less energy than PoW and does not require specialized hardware, making it "greener" and easier for newcomers to enter.

Introduction to Proof of Stake

In Proof of Stake, the blockchain's own cryptocurrency is the scarce resource used to limit users' control over the blockchain. The more cryptocurrency a user owns, the more control they can exert over the block creation process.

Proof of Stake works a lot like buying stock in a company. If you own stock in a company, you have the potential to receive dividends proportional to the amount of stock you own.

In Proof of Stake, a user can stake some of their cryptocurrency, meaning that they promise not to spend it and send it to a special address. As long as that cryptocurrency remains staked, the user has the opportunity to be selected to create blocks. The user can withdraw their stake at any time but loses the ability to be selected as a block creator.

The algorithms used to select Proof of Stake block creators fall into two groups: randomized block selection and coin-age-based selection. The main distinction is the probability of a user being selected to create blocks. In randomized block selection, this probability is proportional to the percentage of the total amount of staked cryptocurrency that the user owns. In coin-age-based selection, both the size of the user's stake and the time since the last time the user created a block are taken into account.

All implementations of Proof of Stake must be capable of performing the block creator selection process in a decentralized and secure manner. Centralization defeats the purpose of blockchain, and an insecure block creator selection process could allow a user to game the system. To accomplish this, the calculation of the next block creator takes several inputs (the hash of the previous block, stake sizes, coin ages, etc.) and passes them through a function that involves a hash calculation. Since all inputs are known to all users, anyone can perform the calculation. However, the use of the previous block hash and a hash function make it difficult for someone to game the system since they can't predict what allocation of stakes across multiple accounts would give them an advantage in time to make the necessary adjustments.

Variants of Proof of Stake

Multiple different variants of Proof of Stake exist. Chain-based Proof of Stake uses stake to directly select block creators and the longest chain rule to determine which of two competing versions of the blockchain is the correct one. We'll focus on this version in this chapter.

Another version of Proof of Stake is called BFT-style Proof of Stake. This variant uses a multistage consensus protocol where a randomly selected block producer proposed a block and the rest of the staked validators vote on whether to accept it. This can enable them to achieve transaction finalization, unlike the probabilistic finalization offered by consensus algorithms using the longest chain rule.

Delegated Proof of Stake (DPoS) implements representative democracy using staked assets. Stakeholders vote for delegates, and a certain number of candidates with the most votes are selected. In this scheme, delegates perform the work of block production and pass rewards down to stakers.

Security of Proof of Stake

The security of Proof of Stake relies on the security of the block creator selection process and digital signatures. For the block creator selection process to be secure, it needs to be impossible for someone to predict block creators in advance and modify their stake to improve their probability of being selected. Proof of Stake uses hash functions to assure this, so the security of Proof of

Stake relies on the security of hash functions. Namely, hash functions must be pseudorandom (to prevent prediction of future states) and one way (to prevent someone reverse-engineering a winning solution).

Digital signature security is also vital to the security of Proof of Stake blockchains. Unlike Proof of Work, where creating a valid block is difficult, creating a valid block in Proof of Stake is very easy. Proof of Stake relies on the fact that users will only accept a block created by the chosen block creator. The authenticity of a block is protected by a digital signature, so digital signatures must be secure and unforgeable for a Proof of Stake blockchain to be secure.

As with Proof of Work, the goal of many attacks against Proof of Stake is to enable double-spend attacks on the blockchain. In the following sections, we'll discuss five methods by which an attacker can gain control of the blockchain, be incentivized to allow a double-spend attack, or perform a denial-of-service attack against blockchain nodes.

XX% Attack

The XX% attack is the Proof of Stake equivalent of the 51% attack in Proof of Work. In this attack, the malicious user accumulates enough of the scarce resource, in this case cryptocurrency, to have a high probability of being chosen as the creator of each new block.

Unlike with Proof of Work, owning 51 percent of the staked cryptocurrency does not guarantee control of the distributed ledger, but it provides a 51 percent chance of being selected to create each block. In order to launch an effective double-spend attack, the attacker needs to control enough of the staked cryptocurrency to have a high probability of being selected as the block creator for the desired number of continuous blocks (typically at least three).

The exact percentage of the staked cryptocurrency needed to perform this attack depends on the desired probability that the attack will succeed. This can be modeled using the equation:

$$S = P^{1/N}$$

where S is the percentage of the stake pool that the attacker needs to control in order to achieve a probability, P, of success in being chosen to create N consecutive blocks that the attacker needs to control in order to launch a successful attack. For reference, a 90 percent probability of success in controlling three blocks requires control of over 96 percent of the stake. The attacker has to decide on an acceptable probability of failure since it is unlikely that they will ever control all of the staked coins.

Countermeasures

In the original Proof of Stake algorithms, "staking" simply referred to owning a cryptocurrency, which meant no penalty existed for misbehavior. The logic was that an attacker would devalue the cryptocurrency, which would hurt the attacker as well.

Modern Proof of Stake algorithms require stakers to deposit their cryptocurrency at a special address to participate in consensus. This gives these algorithms the ability to penalize nodes that misbehave, such as creating divergent versions of the blockchain.

Proof of Stake "Time Bomb"

The Proof of Stake "time bomb" refers to the fact that the user with the highest percentage of stake on the blockchain will eventually be able to perform an XX% attack without any malicious action. This is due to the fact that this user can take advantage of "compounding interest" by staking all cryptocurrency that they earn through block rewards.

In Proof of Stake, the percentage of block rewards that a user earns is proportional to the percentage of the total set of staked coins that they own. The user with the largest percentage of the stake will earn the largest block reward, allowing their stake to grow the most quickly.

As a result, their percentage of the total stake will grow over time, allowing them to earn greater and greater block rewards. Eventually, either the cryptocurrency will die (since all coin is tied up in users' stakes) or the controlling player will own all of the stake (as other users give up their stakes in order to use the coins in transactions).

Countermeasures

This is more of a theoretical attack than a practical one. Accumulating a controlling stake in a Proof of Stake blockchain via block rewards would take a very long time. Also, if an attacker controlled enough of a blockchain's cryptocurrency to make this attack possible, most or all of the blockchain's other users would likely have abandoned it, devaluing the currency and making the attack pointless.

Long-Range Attack

A long-range attack is designed to allow a user without the largest stake in a Proof of Stake blockchain to still take advantage of the "time bomb" effect. In this attack, the attacker chooses a point in the history of the blockchain (typically the genesis block) where they control some of the stake and creates a divergent blockchain.

On the main blockchain, they decline every opportunity they have to create a block. As a result, the main blockchain grows more slowly since any blocks that they fail to create are skipped. This decreases the throughput of the blockchain and is crucial to the attack. The attacker's ability to affect the main blockchain will decrease over time though, since they are earning no new block rewards and their percentage of the total stake is likely shrinking as a result.

On the attacker's version of the blockchain, they create a block whenever possible. As a result, they are the only one earning block rewards, which they reinvest as stake. In the long run, they achieve the same control over the blockchain as the "time bomb."

The challenge in this attack is getting the attacker's version of the blockchain accepted as the official version. To do so, they need their version to contain more blocks than the official one. Unless they own more than half of the stake at the beginning, their version of the chain will grow more slowly at first. Over time, their ability to create blocks on their side chain will increase and eventually surpass the main chain since the main chain will miss any blocks that they are chosen to create as well as occasional ones due to natural errors (chosen block creator failing to create a block within their window). As a result, they will eventually close the gap and become the longest chain, completing the attack.

Countermeasures

A long-range attack exploits the longest chain rule that governs how nodes should treat conflicting versions of the blockchain. In theory, all nodes in the network should accept the malicious version of the blockchain, providing the attacker with complete control over the network and its ledger.

In practice, the nodes in the blockchain are more likely to simply reject the alternative blockchain as obviously malicious even if it should be accepted under the longest chain rule. While this breaks the rules of blockchain, it would enable the blockchain to continue to function.

Resource Exhaustion Attacks

Proof of Stake blockchains require more work to validate than Proof of Work ones. In a Proof of Work blockchain, it is possible to perform a high-level validation of a potential blockchain by verifying the chain of block headers. A valid chain is hard to compute but easy to verify. As a result, nodes can check the chain as an initial verification step before validating each transaction to check that a divergent blockchain is completely legitimate.

In Proof of Stake, the validity of the blockchain depends on the allocation of stake and whether each block is created by the appropriate block producer. As a result, a divergent blockchain is relatively easy to create but hard to verify because it requires access to block bodies to identify and track the staking and unstaking of cryptocurrency.

As a result, fake versions of the blockchain can be used to perform resource exhaustion attacks on chain-based Proof of Stake blockchains. Under the longest chain rule, a node is obligated to determine if a potentially longer chain is valid and to build on it if it is. An attacker who sends invalid divergent blockchains to a node can waste its resources and potentially slow the creation of new blocks due to resources being diverted to inspecting the invalid chain.

Countermeasures

These resource exhaustion attacks take advantage of the design and rules of chain-based Proof of Stake blockchains to attack nodes. Some heuristics exist to determine if a blockchain is likely to be valid before performing an in-depth inspection; however, many of these are vulnerable to attack.[6]

Nothing at Stake Problem

The Nothing at Stake problem in Proof of Stake refers to the fact that there is no incentive in many blockchain systems for block creators not to misbehave. If a fork occurs in the blockchain, whether accidentally or due to an attacker's double-spend attack, there is no mechanism to prevent a block creator from adding a block to both versions of the blockchain.

In fact, doing so is the best move for them. By adding their block to both versions of the blockchain, a block creator guarantees that they will receive their block reward no matter which version of the blockchain eventually is selected as the official one via the longest block rule. Choosing one or the other runs the risk of guessing wrong and having their legitimate block dropped from the ledger.

Countermeasures

The Nothing at Stake problem assumes that validators have no incentive not to build on multiple versions of the blockchain. Some Proof of Stake blockchains, such as Ethereum 2.0, require nodes to send a security deposit to a particular address to be considered as a potential block creator.

This security deposit provides a mechanism for these blockchains to punish nodes that break the rules. If a Proof of Stake validator creates blocks on conflicting chains, they may lose part of their stake or be ejected as a validator entirely.

Case Studies

Since the launch of Ethereum 2.0, multiple nodes have been penalized for signing multiple conflicting versions of blocks. Often, this is due to configuration errors and restarting nodes, but some attempts may have been malicious.

One example is the "slashing" of 75 Eth2 validators operated by Staked, a staking infrastructure provider.[7] These nodes unexpectedly restarted due to configuration changes and mistakenly signed an alternative version of a previously signed block. As a result, the nodes incurred a penalty of 18 ETH worth $29,000 at the time.

Threat Modeling for Consensus

Most blockchain consensus attacks are designed to help an attacker achieve a 51% attack or otherwise increase their control over the digital ledger. The following list includes some of the impacts of these attacks mapped to the STRIDE threat model:

- **Tampering:** 51% attacks allow the digital ledger to be rewritten, breaking blockchain immutability.

- **Repudiation:** 51% attacks permit double-spend attacks that allow an attacker to overwrite and repudiate past transactions.

- **Denial of Service:** An attacker can artificially raise the difficulty threshold of a Proof of Work blockchain, slowing block creation. A 51% attacker can refuse to add transactions to the blockchain, blocking them from being added to the digital ledger.

- **Elevation of Privileges:** 51%, long-range, selfish mining, and SPV mining attacks are designed to provide an attacker with complete or elevated control over the state of the digital ledger.

Block Creation

The blockchain is designed to be a distributed, decentralized ledger. Each node in the blockchain network has the ability to store a complete copy of the blockchain. This makes it necessary to have a formalized method of updating the ledger so that the network can remain synchronized.

Blockchain achieves this by collecting individual transactions into blocks and updating the ledger a block at a time. The blockchain protocol is designed to perform these updates at (near) regular intervals, making it possible to predict how quickly information will be added to the distributed ledger.

Stages of Block Creation

Adding a new block to the distributed ledger is a multistage process. The five main stages of ledger update are as follows:

- Transaction transmission
- Block creator selection (consensus)
- Block building
- Block transmission
- Block validation

Each of these stages is important to the effectiveness and security of the blockchain's distributed ledger.

Transaction Transmission

The first stage of the block creation process happens continuously. In this stage, people who are using the blockchain system generate transactions and transmit them to their peers in the blockchain network.

For example, a Bitcoin user may generate and digitally sign a transaction before sending it to the nodes in the network that the user is directly connected to. Upon receipt of this transaction, these nodes send it on to their peers, allowing it to propagate across the network.

At the time of transmission, this transaction is not considered part of the distributed ledger. Nodes maintain a pool of pending transactions that have not yet been included in blocks. When the time comes to create a block, the block creator will draw from this pool to create the next piece of the distributed ledger.

Block Creator Selection (Consensus)

This stage of the block creation process uses the consensus algorithms described earlier to select the creator of the next block. The blockchain network has no central authority that determines the contents of each block; however, it needs someone to create the official version of the block that the rest of the network will accept. The blockchain consensus algorithm ensures that this is completed in a decentralized fashion to ensure that no one can control the blockchain's ledger.

This step may fall earlier or later in the block creation process depending on the consensus algorithm used by the blockchain. In Proof of Work, the block needs to be created before consensus is completed since the criteria for becoming the block creator is the ability to generate a valid block. In Proof of Stake, the choice of block creator is not dependent on the contents of the block, so it is completed before the new block is built.

Block Building

The chosen block creator has a couple of responsibilities. The first is to put together a block that meets the requirements of the blockchain (maximum size, etc.). The second is to ensure that the block is a valid one.

When generating a new block, block creators have complete control over its contents. Many blockchains include the concept of transaction fees, where users can pay for their transaction to be prioritized when a new block is created. A greedy block creator should create a block with the highest possible transaction fees since they receive fees included in their blocks; however, there is no obligation to do so. For this reason, block creators have a great deal of power in the blockchain network, which is why it is so important that the system remains decentralized.

The other important responsibility of block creators is ensuring the validity of the blocks that they create. One of the main threats in blockchain is a double-spend attack, where a user creates mutually conflicting transactions (i.e., sends the same cryptocurrency to two different recipients). The creator of a block is obliged to ensure that their block does not create any double spends within the ledger. Failure to do so risks a future block creator choosing not to build on top of their block, orphaning it and denying the block creator the rewards that they receive for creating the block.

Block Transmission

Once a block has been completed, its creator digitally signs it and transmits it to the rest of the blockchain network. This mimics the process of transaction transmission, where each node in the network transmits it to their peers once they receive it.

Block Validation

Finally, each node in the network needs to validate a block before adding it to their official copy of the distributed ledger. The consensus algorithm attempts to ensure that only one node in the network creates a block, but it doesn't guarantee that the node is not malicious. Each node in the network performs the same search for double-spends that the block creator should have done and accepts the block only if it meets all of the blockchain's requirements.

Attacking Block Creation

The block creation process is essential to updating the distributed ledger and making the blockchain function. However, the design of this process leaves it vulnerable to attacks on the blockchain's availability and the integrity of the data that it contains.

Denial of Service

A denial-of-service attack is a common type of attack against any system. By overwhelming some component of the system's ability to process inputs, it degrades or destroys the effectiveness of the system as a whole. While blockchain's decentralization makes it immune to some types of denial-of-service attacks, others are still possible.

One type of denial-of-service attack that targets the block creation process involves transaction flooding. By creating a large number of spam transactions and posting them to the blockchain, an attacker can have both short-term and long-term impacts on the blockchain's functioning.

In the short term, transaction flooding impacts the ability of legitimate transactions to be added to the distributed ledger. Blockchains often have set block sizes and block rates, meaning they have a set maximum capacity. If an attacker's spam transactions take up any part of this capacity, it reduces the ability of the blockchain to process legitimate transactions.

One way that blockchains combat spam transactions is by including transaction fees, making an attacker pay to attack the blockchain. However, if an attacker is undeterred by the cost, this can have another short-term impact on the blockchain. In order to have their transactions added to the ledger during an attack, legitimate users will have to pay higher fees for priority. Increasing the cost of using the system decreases its usability.

The potential long-term impact of this attack is bloat on the blockchain. A crucial feature of blockchain technology is its immutability, meaning that every transaction that makes it onto the ledger must be stored forever (and checked during validation). Every spam transaction that makes it onto the distributed ledger makes the system that much less usable.

This is only one form of denial-of-service attack that can impact the block creation process. Block creation can also be disrupted by any attack that inhibits the creation, transmission, or validation of blocks, such as a distributed denial-of-service (DDoS) attack against the block creator or an attempt to disrupt communications over the peer-to-peer network.

Countermeasures

Protection against these types of denial-of-service attacks requires individual action by the affected nodes. For example, block creators can refuse to include spam transactions in their blocks, keeping them from affecting the digital ledger, and deploy DDoS mitigation solutions.

However, these approaches have their challenges, such as differentiating legitimate from spam transactions. Additionally, this requires relying on a particular node to protect the blockchain, which violates blockchain's goals of decentralization and not requiring trust in other nodes.

Case Studies

The Solana blockchain has suffered from repeated incidents that may be transaction flooding DDoS attacks or legitimate traffic overwhelming the network.[8] These incidents take advantage of the fact that the Solana blockchain has extremely low transaction fees (0.00025 per transaction), making it affordable to flood the blockchain network with spam transactions.

Other blockchains have experienced DDoS attacks designed to make a profit for the attackers. An attack in March 2020 caused significant congestion on the Ethereum network at the same time that Ether's value decreased significantly. These price decreases caused collateral on the MakerDAO lending platform to be auctioned off. The attackers were able to win auctions with zero-bid transactions because competing bids couldn't get through, netting them $8.3 million.[9]

Frontrunning

In blockchain, the delay between the public transmission of a transaction and its inclusion in the distributed ledger creates the potential for "frontrunning" attacks. A blockchain system can have situations where being the first to submit a solution has a tangible benefit. For example, an auction can be run on the blockchain where, if two bidders have the same maximum that they are willing to bid, whichever one can place their bid first wins.

On blockchain, submitting a bid would require creating and broadcasting a transaction to the network. At the time of broadcast, this transaction is not trusted or considered part of the distributed ledger. Instead, it is stored in a pool of similar, untrusted transactions until the next block is ready to be created. At this point, the block creator will build a block that may contain this transaction and add it to the blockchain.

If this block creator is motivated by self-interest (which blockchain encourages), they will order transactions in the block based upon their associated transaction fees. This means that a transaction created later but with a higher transaction fee will be given priority. Therefore, a participant in the auction who observes the bid transaction and makes the same bid but with a higher transaction fee is likely to be the one seen first and chosen by the auctioneer. On blockchain, the first transaction created isn't necessarily the first one processed.

Countermeasures

Frontrunning attacks take advantage of the fact that transactions are publicized to the blockchain network before they are included within a block. This provides an attacker with a window in which to create a competing transaction that might be added and processed first.

One solution to this problem is exclusive mining, in which a transaction creator only shares a transaction with a single potential block creator. When this node is next selected to create a block, they can include the transaction in it. This prevents frontrunning because the transaction is only made public once it has already been added to the ledger. Unless an attacker performs a 51% attack, there is no way for a frontrunning transaction to come before it.

This approach has been used in the past to protect transactions designed to exploit a vulnerability before a hacker can. In 2020, a white-hat hack of a vulnerability in a Lien Finance smart contract protected over $9.6 million in tokens from being stolen by an attacker.[10] The exploit involved the use of exclusive mining by the SparkPool mining pool to protect against frontrunning attacks.

Case Studies

Frontrunning attacks are common occurrences in the decentralized finance (DeFi) spots. Automated bots scan the pools of pending transactions for trades that they can exploit, frontrunning the transaction to buy low and sell high.

While these bots are designed to exploit other blockchain users, they occasionally end up doing more good than evil. In a hack against the DODO decentralized exchange (DEX), for example, a bot "front ran" transactions by an attacker trying to exploit the vulnerable DEX.[11] Of the $3.8 million in tokens extracted from the protocol, $1.89 million was taken by the bot and later returned to the protocol by the bot's owner.

SPV Mining

SPV mining was mentioned previously since it is an attack against Proof of Work consensus. However, it also applies to the block creation process. SPV miners deliberately skip steps of the block creation process in order to gain an advantage.

A legitimate miner must download a complete copy of each block in the blockchain and then validate that they are not creating double-spends with their new block. An SPV miner skips both of these steps since a block that only contains the miner's block reward can't possibly include a double-spend.

Threat Modeling for Block Creation

Mapping attacks against block creation to the STRIDE threat model highlights the following threats:

- **Tampering:** Frontrunning attacks are designed to allow later transactions to be processed before earlier ones, changing the impacts of these transactions.

- **Denial of Service:** An attacker can perform a denial-of-service attack in various ways, slowing or stopping block creation and the addition of transactions to the digital ledger.

- **Elevation of Privileges:** SPV mining provides an attacker with an increased probability of creating blocks and greater control over the contents of the digital ledger.

Conclusion

The blockchain protocols define the theory of blockchain. Consensus algorithms describe how mutually distrusting blockchain nodes work together to choose block producers, and the block creation protocol outlines how the network will organize and validate transactions to update the blockchain's ledger.

In the next chapter, we'll move on from theory to practice. Blockchain systems are implemented as software that runs on computers and communicates over modern networks. This underlying infrastructure introduces new security considerations and potential attack vectors.

Notes

1. https://lamport.azurewebsites.net/pubs/byz.pdf

2. https://hacked.slowmist.io/en/?c=Blockchain

3. https://blog.theabacus.io/the-verge-hack-explained-7942f63a3017

4. https://decrypt.co/3506/spy-mining-hits-ethereum

5. https://decrypt.co/3506/spy-mining-hits-ethereum

6. https://medium.com/@dsl_uiuc/fake-stake-attacks-on-chain-based-proof-of-stake-cryptocurrencies-b8b05723f806

7. https://cointelegraph.com/news/expensive-lesson-75-eth2-validators-slashed-for-introducing-potential-chain-split-bug

8. https://cryptonews.com/news/solana-reportedly-went-down-again-after-ddos-attack.htm

9. www.coindesk.com/tech/2020/07/22/mempool-manipulation-enabled-theft-of-8m-in-makerdao-collateral-on-black-thursday-report

10. https://samczsun.com/escaping-the-dark-forest

11. https://dodoexhelp.zendesk.com/hc/en-us/articles/900004851126-Important-update-regarding-recent-events-on-DODO

Infrastructure

Chapter 3 explored blockchains at the theoretical, protocol level. Like HTTP, these protocols define how different systems should interact to achieve a particular goal.

While the blockchain theory described in a blockchain's white paper fully defines how the system should work, blockchains need to be implemented to be usable. This creates a reliance on underlying infrastructure.

Blockchain protocols can be implemented in various different ways. For example, Bitcoin could be run using pen, paper, and carrier pigeon; however, this approach would create a very slow and unusable system.

Blockchain technology relies on modern IT equipment. This includes implementing blockchain as software running on blockchain nodes and communicating over computer networks.

Nodes

Blockchain systems are implemented as software. This software runs on computers called *nodes*.

While a blockchain may have very strong security at the theoretical level, implementing the protocols as code introduces additional risks. Blockchain software could contain business logic or implementation errors or be vulnerable to attacks by other software operating within the same environment.

Inside a Blockchain Node

A blockchain node is just software running on a computer. However, a blockchain node may have many different responsibilities. The following roles are among those that a blockchain node may fulfill:

- **Ledger Storage:** Every node in the blockchain network can maintain a copy of the blockchain's digital ledger. This requires the ability to store the contents of the ledger and access the contents of transactions or blocks as needed.

- **Block Production:** The blockchain's digital ledger is updated by blocks containing collections of transactions. A blockchain node may participate in the consensus process and the creation and distribution of block candidates.

- **Block Validation:** Blockchains are designed to perform decentralized validation of the transactions stored on the blockchain's digital ledger. A blockchain node is expected to validate each block it receives before adding the block to its copy of the digital ledger.

- **Smart Contract Execution:** Smart contract platforms allow programs to run on top of the digital ledger. Nodes in a smart contract platform host a virtual machine and execute code within it as part of the process of validating blocks and updating the digital ledger.

Not every node in the blockchain network fulfills all of these roles. For example, a node may elect not to participate in consensus and block production.

However, meeting the needs of the blockchain network requires significant resources on behalf of the blockchain node. Attacks against these nodes that disrupt access to these resources can have significant impacts on the performance and security of the blockchain network.

Attacking Blockchain Nodes

Blockchain nodes can be attacked in various different ways. In the following sections, I'll cover some of the primary threats to the security of blockchain nodes and their users:

- Blockchain-specific malware
- Denial-of-service attacks

- Failure to update
- Malicious inputs
- Software misconfigurations

Blockchain-Specific Malware

Blockchain software running on a node is also running alongside other software, including both legitimate programs and potential malware.

Some malware variants are specifically designed to target blockchain systems. Some of the potential effects of these malware variants are as follows:

- **Theft of Private Keys:** Malware installed on a node or blockchain user's computer may monitor the clipboard and scan the computer's memory for data that resembles blockchain private keys. The keys can then be exfiltrated to the attacker, providing full control over the user's account.

- **Transaction Modification:** Blockchain malware may be designed to make changes to transaction data before it is digitally signed by a user. For example, malware may replace the destination address of a transaction with that of the attacker or modify transactions to create malicious approvals for attackers to extract a user's tokens from decentralized finance (DeFi) projects.

- **Traffic Filtering:** A blockchain node's view of the state of the blockchain and ability to participate in its operations depend on its ability to receive and send transactions and blocks. Malware that intercepts and filters a node's blockchain traffic could feed it a false version of the state of the blockchain. This could trick the user into supporting a divergent blockchain that supports an attacker's 51% attack.

- **Denial-of-Service Attacks:** Malware running on a node could perform a denial-of-service attack on that node. This could be accomplished by consuming resources, attacking the blockchain software process, or other means.

The security of a blockchain account and the blockchain network as a whole depends on the security of the blockchain software running on nodes. Malware installed on these nodes could disrupt their operation in various ways.

Countermeasures
Malware infections are a traditional IT security threat, and blockchain-specific malware is not very different from other variants. Traditional anti-malware solutions can help to protect against this threat.

Case Studies

The Tron blockchain was vulnerable to DoS attacks due to the use of big decimals in the code.[1] Each load of a big decimal takes 2 to 3 minutes on a modern laptop and the code used 6 big decimals per request. An attacker exploiting this vulnerability could tie up a Tron node's CPU and also fill up its memory, making the blockchain software unusable.

Denial-of-Service Attacks

Denial-of-service (DoS) attacks can occur at most levels of the blockchain ecosystem. At the node level, a denial-of-service attack involves crashing the blockchain software running on an individual node.

DoS attacks can be performed against a node in various different ways. A node may be the victim of a distributed denial-of-service (DDoS) attack that overwhelms it with spam traffic and renders it unable to respond to legitimate requests. Malware installed on a node could consume memory or computational resources to hinder blockchain-related processes. Blockchain transactions may be specially crafted to consume resources and crash blockchain nodes.

A DoS attack can hurt both the blockchain node and the network as a whole. A blockchain node targeted by a DoS attack may no longer be able to participate in the blockchain network. The loss of this node could also impact the security and performance of the blockchain network by rendering it unable to participate in consensus and block production.

Countermeasures

Denial-of-service attacks can come from both inside and outside the blockchain ecosystem. Nodes can deploy traditional anti-DDoS and anti-malware solutions to protect against external threats. Inside the blockchain ecosystem, systems must be designed to protect against malicious transactions designed to consume resources and overwhelm blockchain nodes.

Case Studies

Denial-of-service attacks have been performed multiple different times against blockchain networks by exploiting software flaws. A flaw in the Bitcoin Core codebase enabled an attacker to either perform a denial-of-service attack against nodes or inflate the cryptocurrency by using the same Bitcoin in multiple transactions.[2] This vulnerability was enabled by poor code review of the Bitcoin Core software and was patched before it was exploited on the Bitcoin blockchain. However, other blockchains forked the Bitcoin Core software and were vulnerable to the same attacks as a result. The Pigeoncoin cryptocurrency became famous as a blockchain attacked using this vulnerability, enabling the attacker to print 235 million Pigeoncoins (nearly a quarter of the intended maximum supply).

Failure to Update

Blockchain software is software, and all software occasionally needs updates. The updates may be designed to add functionality or correct issues identified with earlier releases.

Update and patch management is a significant challenge in the traditional IT space. This leads to attackers scanning for and exploiting publicly known vulnerabilities for which patches are available.

However, blockchain decentralization exacerbates the update and patch management process. The security of the blockchain network depends on the security of the nodes in the network, but no centralized authority exists with the power to compel nodes to make updates.

This problem is exacerbated by the fact that some updates to blockchain protocols may be controversial. For example, Bitcoin Cash forked from Bitcoin over the SegWit upgrade, and Ethereum Classic diverged due to Ethereum's response to the DAO hack.

Blockchain nodes face several update-related security risks:

- **Node Exploitation:** Some blockchain software updates are designed to correct security vulnerabilities that place blockchain nodes at risk. If a node fails to install an update, it may be exploited by an attacker.

- **Blockchain Forks:** Blockchain is governed by the longest chain rule, which states that the longest version of two conflicting versions of the blockchain should be accepted. If an update contains a hard fork, nodes that have and have not installed the update may follow different blockchain forks. This can cause disruption and increases a blockchain network's exposure to consensus attacks.

- **Malicious Updates:** Blockchain software is commonly developed under an open-source model with contributions accepted from third parties. Attackers may insert malicious functionality into blockchain code that is distributed as part of a software update.

Software updates are essential to maintaining the security of the blockchain and expanding its functionality. However, often blockchain developers need to walk a fine line between encouraging nodes to install updates and publicizing vulnerabilities when enough blockchain nodes are vulnerable that attacks could disrupt the functioning of the blockchain network.

Countermeasures

Blockchain software often operates under Linus's law, which states that "given enough eyeballs, all bugs are shallow." However, this only applies if qualified developers actually audit the code. Blockchain software should follow secure development practices to ensure that updates are high quality, and nodes should install updates as soon as they are available.

Case Studies

The Ethereum Parity client had an integer overflow vulnerability up to version 2.2.10 that would allow an attacker to remotely crash Parity nodes.[3] A month after the vulnerability was announced, 40 percent of Parity nodes still had not applied the patch. These nodes represented 15 percent of all Ethereum nodes at the time, so exploitation of the vulnerability could have had a noticeable impact on the performance and security of the Ethereum network.

Malicious Inputs

Blockchain software is designed to process untrusted input. Users have the ability to submit transactions to the blockchain that will be processed and possibly executed by the blockchain software.

Ideally, all of this processing is performed within the blockchain's isolated virtual machine. However, if the code that processes transactions, smart contract code, or blocks contains a vulnerability, an attacker may be able to exploit it to attack the blockchain network or break out of the sandboxed blockchain environment.

These injection attacks can have significant impacts on a node or the rest of the network. A blockchain breakout could allow an attacker to access the underlying host, potentially causing it to crash or allowing the attacker to take it over.

Attacks on blockchain nodes could also affect the blockchain network as a whole. For example, exploitation of a DoS vulnerability that causes vulnerable nodes to crash could make it easier for an attacker to perform a 51% attack against the network due to the significant reduction in the network's hashpower.

Countermeasures

Malicious inputs and injection vulnerabilities are enabled by poor input validation. Any code that accepts and processes untrusted user input should verify that the input is valid before processing it.

Case Studies

This sort of attack could have happened to users of the EOS distributed ledger software. Pre-launch, researchers from security firm Qihoo 360 examined the EOS source code and identified a failure to correctly check the bounds of an array before writing to it.[4] This vulnerability was in the code that parsed EOS transactions, meaning that it would be exploitable by a malicious EOS user. The researchers ethically reported it to the EOS team, and it was corrected.

The impact of this vulnerability would allow an attacker to write code anywhere within the running EOS code. The Qihoo researchers developed proof of concept attacks demonstrating that it was possible to use the vulnerability to generate a reverse shell. This would allow the attacker to gain control over the affected computer with the same permissions as the EOS process. Since every node in a blockchain network would process all transactions included in a block, getting a malicious transaction included in a block would allow an attacker to exploit all nodes in the EOS network.

Software Misconfigurations

Blockchain software can contain a great deal of optional functionality. For example, blockchain nodes may have the opportunity to connect with external applications for managing private keys, performing transactions, and so on.

With these optional features comes the risk that users may enable them without knowing or considering the security implications. For example, the ability to connect to external systems that can make transactions using a blockchain account is great for an order processing or logistics management system but a major problem if accessed by an attacker.

Countermeasures

Optional features in blockchain software should be disabled by default. Before enabling any features, users should research their purpose, how they work, and best practices for using and securing them.

Case Studies

An example of attackers taking advantage of this sort of tinkering is a series of thefts from Ethereum wallets.[5] This wallet software had the ability to open up port 8545 to allow external software to interact with the wallet via remote procedure calls (RPCs). This feature is designed to allow the wallet to be integrated with an organization's software that would be empowered to perform transactions on the Ethereum blockchain.

The feature is designed to be used internally, so users should block port 8545 at the network firewall to prevent exploitation. The feature is disabled by default, but some hobbyists enabled it without knowing the appropriate security precautions to take. As a result, over $20 million in Ether was stolen from Ethereum users by attackers that scanned for port 8545 being open on vulnerable devices.

Threat Modeling for Blockchain Nodes

Blockchain nodes have security threats that cover all of the STRIDE categories except repudiation:

- **Spoofing:** Blockchain malware can steal private keys or modify transactions to perform actions on behalf of a blockchain account.

- **Tampering:** Malware can be used to perform eclipse/routing attacks, which can enable 51% attacks and rewriting of the history of the distributed ledger.

- **Information Disclosure:** Theft of private keys by blockchain malware can allow the attacker to decrypt messages intended for the account owner.

- **Denial of Service:** Blockchain nodes can suffer DoS attacks in various ways, such as malware attacks or not being able to access the blockchain after a hard fork due to a failure to apply updates.

- **Elevation of Privileges:** Blockchain malware can steal private keys, providing unauthorized access to a user's account. Exploitation of injection vulnerabilities with malicious inputs could provide an attacker with access to or control over the underlying node.

Networks

Blockchain nodes must be able to communicate with one another. Nodes need access to the latest transactions and blocks in order to perform updates to their copies of the blockchain's distributed ledger.

Decentralization is a core tenet of blockchain, so blockchain networks do not operate under a client-server model. Instead, blockchains use a peer-to-peer network where each node is directly connected to a few other nodes. Information percolates across the blockchain via multiple different hops. Any pair of nodes has multiple different paths linking them, making blockchain networks highly redundant and resilient.

Reliable, high-performance communications are essential to blockchain consensus and the synchronization of the blockchain network. For this reason, the security of the underlying network infrastructure that blockchain relies upon can have a significant impact on the security of the blockchain protocol itself.

Attacking the Blockchain Network

Blockchain networks can be attacked in a few different ways. The impacts of these attacks range from disruptions and degraded performance to the potential for double-spends and attacks on blockchain consensus. Three types of network-level attacks against the blockchain are as follows:

- Denial of service
- Eclipse/routing
- Sybil

Denial-of-service Attacks

As a distributed, decentralized system, blockchains are supposed to be immune to traditional denial-of-service (DoS) attacks. In a traditional DoS attack, the attacker attempts to overwhelm a single point of failure or bottleneck in the system, resulting in degraded functionality. For example, many real-world DoS attacks attempt to flood a webserver with connection attempts. Once the webserver's connection capacity is exceeded, it can no longer accept legitimate connections.

In a fully decentralized blockchain, there is no central authority operating the network, so no permanent single point of failure exists. However, temporary single points of failure exist in many blockchain implementations, and some implementations are not fully decentralized. Either of these enable DoS attacks to be performed against the system.

An example of a temporary single point of failure is the block creator selected by the blockchain consensus algorithm. These algorithms are designed to ensure that only a single person can be selected to create a block within a given interval. If an attacker can predict the next block creator before they have the opportunity to generate and distribute a block (which is definitely possible in Proof of Stake), they can DoS that user. At a minimum, distribution of the block may be delayed, and the block may even be ignored if it is not published within the appropriate interval.

While the original blockchain had no permanent single points of failure, modifications have been made to the protocol to create them in some instances. All private and permissioned blockchain implementations have some level of centralization since someone has the ability to allow/deny access to the blockchain network or elevated privileges on the network. Examples of these single points of failure (which can be DoSed) include membership service providers (MSPs) on the Hyperledger private blockchain and the use of masternodes on a variety of permissioned blockchains.

Countermeasures

DoS attacks against block producers and other single points of failure in blockchain networks use traditional methods to degrade or destroy the availability of these systems. Anti-DDoS, anti-malware, and similar solutions can help to protect a node against these attacks.

Case Studies

To perform a DoS attack against a block producer or other node critical to the blockchain's operation, it is necessary to unmask the identity of that node. However, this is easier than it should be. In a 2018 talk at Devcon 4, Péter Szilágyi outlined a few ways in which the identity of Ethereum users can be revealed, including trackers and the discovery protocol used to connect light nodes to the network.[6] With information on nodes' IP addresses and locations, it is possible to target them for DDoS and other attacks.

Eclipse/Routing Attacks

An important assumption for blockchain security is that all nodes in the network have a connection to one another, either directly or through a series of peer connections. In an eclipse or routing attack, an attacker deliberately isolates one or more nodes from the rest of the blockchain network. This isolation allows the attacker to affect the targeted nodes' view of the state of the blockchain ecosystem and can be used as part of several different attacks.

Figure 4.1 illustrates an eclipse/routing attack on the blockchain. The malicious node in the center of the image controls all routes of communication between two segments of the blockchain network. This allows the node to control data flowing between these two segments.

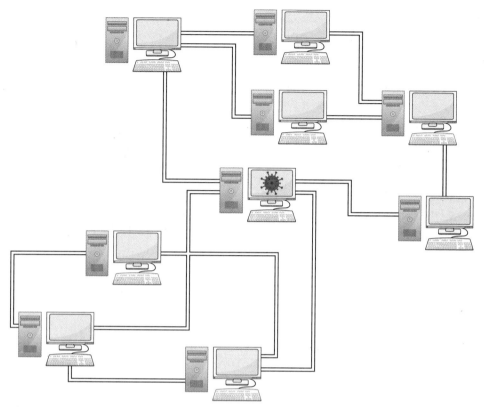

Figure 4.1: Routing attack

One simple use of an eclipse/routing attack is performing a double-spend attack. By sending different versions of the same transaction to each isolated segment of the network, the attacker can get users in those segments to accept and act upon the version they see. When the attack is completed, the isolated segments will reconnect and find that they have conflicting versions of history. Under the longest chain rule, the shorter version will be discarded, leaving only one version of the conflicting transactions in the official history of the network. Since the attacker controls how and for how long the network is split, they can ensure that the longer chain contains the version of history they prefer.

Eclipse/routing attacks can also be used to make a 51% attack easier to perform. If one isolated segment only has 60 percent of the network's hashpower, then the attacker only needs to control 30 percent of the hashpower to create the accepted version of the blockchain in that segment. Once the attacker's version is accepted and endorsed by that 60 percent and becomes the longest overall chain, the attacker can end the eclipse/routing attack. The attacker's version of the blockchain would then be accepted by the entire network.

Eclipse and routing attacks can be performed through a variety of different means. If the attack is targeting a single user (an eclipse attack), malware or a Sybil attack can be used to control the victim's connection to the rest of the blockchain network. If malware controls a node's network connection or the attacker controls enough Sybil accounts that all of a node's peers are malicious, then the attacker can filter the node's view of the blockchain network.

A means of partitioning groups of nodes from one another (a routing attack) is through a Border Gateway Protocol (BGP) hijack. BGP is designed to define paths between autonomous systems (ASs)—such as an ISP's network—on the Internet, and an AS will implicitly trust the authenticity of provided routes to a set of IP addresses. If an attacker successfully spoofs a BGP route that is shorter than all legitimate ones, it will be the one selected. As a result, all traffic between two peers (or even two sets of IP prefixes) will pass through the attacker's control before reaching its destination. This allows an attacker to manipulate the topology of the blockchain network, severing links between segments to isolate them except through attacker-controlled nodes.

Countermeasures

Eclipse and routing attacks depend on the attacker's ability to break the blockchain network into multiple, isolated segments. Nodes can make this more difficult by deliberately selecting distributed peers, using multihomed nodes connected to different IP prefixes, and analyzing network statistics for slowdowns caused by a sudden loss of hashpower due to network partitioning.

Case Studies

A 2017 study found that routing attacks would be relatively easy to perform due to the distribution of Bitcoin nodes over the Internet.[7] At the time, 60 percent of Bitcoin network traffic passed through three ISPs.

The prevalence of BGP routing attacks meant that Bitcoin nodes were often impacted by these attacks. In fact, at least 100 nodes had traffic rerouted by BGP hijacking attacks in each month between October 2015 and March 2016, and approximately 8 percent of Bitcoin nodes were impacted by an attack in November 2015.

Sybil Attacks

Sybil attacks are simple network-level attacks designed to facilitate other types of attacks. In a Sybil attack, the attacker creates a large number of user accounts on the blockchain. Figure 4.2 illustrates a Sybil attack.

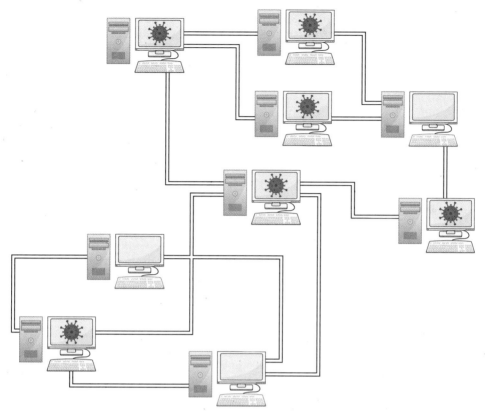

Figure 4.2: Sybil attack

Sybil attacks differ from 51% attacks in that each Sybil account doesn't necessarily have to have a large number of computational resources at its disposal. In fact, Sybil nodes can be an important component of different attacks simply by acting as an active account that relays received blocks and transactions to its peers.

A common example of a Sybil attack is a malicious blockchain user attempting to exploit a poorly designed on-chain governance system. If, in on-chain voting, every account on the blockchain network gets a vote, then an attacker can control the governance system by creating a large number of dummy accounts to participate in voting. For this reason, many blockchain systems using on-chain governance allocate voting power based upon the user's stake in the network, either directly or by defining certain users as masternodes based upon their ownership of a certain, minimum amount of the blockchain's cryptocurrency.

Sybil attacks can also be used to facilitate eclipse/routing attacks as shown in Figure 4.2. If an attacker controls a large percentage of a network's accounts and nodes, other nodes are more likely to select a malicious node as a peer. If all routes between two nodes pass through a malicious node, then an attacker has the ability to filter traffic flowing between these nodes.

Countermeasures
Most blockchain consensus and governance algorithms are designed to protect against Sybil attacks by using control of a scarce asset as a proxy for votes. The impacts of Sybil attacks at the network level can be mitigated by following best practices for detecting and mitigating eclipse/routing attacks.

Case Studies
The anonymity of blockchain accounts makes it difficult to detect a Sybil attack. A 2019 study that simulated the effects of a Sybil attack found that Sybil nodes could impact blockchain performance but that malicious nodes could be detected by checking if a node only forwarded transactions or blocks from particular nodes.[8]

Threat Modeling for Blockchain Networks

Attacks on blockchain networks fall into several STRIDE threat categories:

- **Tampering:** Eclipse/routing attacks can help an attacker to perform a 51% attack, which rewrites the history of the distributed ledger.
- **Repudiation:** Eclipse/routing attacks can enable double-spends and 51% attacks, allowing an attacker to repudiate past transactions.
- **Denial of Service:** Blockchain networks can fall victim to denial-of-service attacks in various ways.
- **Elevation of Privileges:** Eclipse/routing attacks can make a 51% achievable, granting the attacker control over the blockchain.

Conclusion

Blockchain nodes and networks constitute the physical infrastructure that transforms theoretical blockchain protocols into workable systems. However, this transition from theory to practice can create additional attack vectors against blockchain systems.

In the next chapter, we'll move beyond the basic blockchain protocol defined and implemented by Bitcoin and similar blockchain networks. Smart contract platforms allow programs to run on top of the blockchain's digital ledger, and blockchain extensions enable blockchain scalability, extensibility, and interoperability.

Notes

1. www.yahoo.com/video/tron-discloses-critical-vulnerability-could-211000583.html

2. www.coindesk.com/markets/2018/10/02/bitcoin-bug-exploited-on-crypto-fork-as-attacker-prints-235-million-pigeoncoins

3. https://cointelegraph.com/news/data-just-2-3-of-eth-nodes-running-parity-have-been-patched-against-critical-security-flaw

4. https://thehackernews.com/2018/05/eos-blockchain-smart-contract.html

5. https://cointelegraph.com/news/ethereum-hacks-on-the-rise-again-as-price-remains-below-100

6. www.coindesk.com/markets/2018/11/08/the-little-known-ways-ethereum-reveals-user-location-data

7. https://btc-hijack.ethz.ch

8. https://ieeexplore.ieee.org/document/8944507

Advanced

Bitcoin, the original blockchain protocol, was primarily designed to implement a decentralized system for tracking financial transactions. While Bitcoin has some scripting capabilities, these programs are not Turing-complete, meaning they cannot implement all of the functionality that a program running on another computer could. This lack of Turing-completeness limits their capabilities.

Smart contract platforms extend the blockchain protocol to allow Turing-complete programs to run on top of the blockchain, dramatically expanding what can be done on the blockchain. Blockchain extensions go a step further, leveraging smart contracts' capabilities to build protocols that address key limitations of blockchain technology by building new protocols on top of them or interconnecting different blockchain systems.

Smart Contracts

Smart contracts are programs that run on top of a blockchain's distributed ledger. The goal of smart contract platforms is to create a "world computer" where each node in the blockchain network maintains an instance of a virtual machine and the state of this virtual machine is synchronized across the blockchain network.

Smart contract platforms achieve synchronization by controlling the instructions that are run on the distributed virtual machine and the execution environment. Instructions are coordinated using the blockchain's distributed ledger and consensus algorithms. Instructions are embedded in transactions, which are organized into blocks and added to the ledger. This ensures that, if the network is in consensus regarding the state of the blockchain, every node agrees on the order in which transactions are executed.

Smart contract platforms control the execution environment by running these instructions in a virtual machine. Smart contracts' virtual machines are designed to create identical, deterministic execution environments on every node in the network.

In theory, if every node runs the same code in identical environments, they should all have the exact same results. This makes it possible to maintain both decentralization and synchronization within the "world computer."

Smart Contract Vulnerabilities

Smart contracts are software, and software has bugs. Even as immature as smart contract technology is, there are a variety of common vulnerabilities already associated with it.

The following sections cover some of the most common smart contract vulnerabilities. However, since the smart contract and smart contract security landscapes are constantly evolving, this will never be a comprehensive list of all possible smart contract vulnerabilities.

In this discussion, vulnerabilities are divided into four major categories:

- **General Programming Vulnerabilities:** These vulnerabilities can exist in any application. Smart contracts contain them simply because they are programs.

- **Blockchain-Specific Vulnerabilities:** These vulnerabilities arise from the unique design of blockchain technology. They are platform-agnostic and apply across most or all blockchain implementations.

- **Platform-Specific Vulnerabilities:** These vulnerabilities are specific to a certain smart contract platform. Ethereum and EOSIO are two of the oldest and most used smart contract platforms, which have provided the most opportunity for vulnerabilities to be discovered.

- **Application-Specific Vulnerabilities:** Smart contracts can be designed for different purposes. Decentralized finance (DeFi) and non-fungible tokens (NFTs) are two of the most common and fastest-growing applications of smart contracts.

General Programming Vulnerabilities

General programming vulnerabilities are vulnerabilities that can exist in any program. They arise from how software works and manages variables, memory, and so on.

A buffer overflow vulnerability is an example of a general programming vulnerability. Programs allocate chunks of memory to hold data, and problems can arise if the data to be placed in the buffer is larger than the buffer itself. As long as programs manage memory in this way, buffer overflows are a potential risk in languages that lack protections against them.

A complete list of all the potential general programming vulnerabilities that could exist in smart contracts is beyond the scope of this discussion. Some of the main vulnerabilities that appear in smart contracts are as follows:

- Arithmetic vulnerabilities
- Decimal precision
- Digital signature vulnerabilities
- External dependencies
- Right-to-left control characters
- Unsafe serialization

Arithmetic Vulnerabilities

Arithmetic vulnerabilities such as integer overflow and underflow vulnerabilities can exist in most programming languages. Arithmetic vulnerabilities are made possible by how variables work.

Variables and Signedness

A variable is a fixed-size chunk of memory designed to hold a value. How the series of bits stored in this variable is interpreted depends on the variable type. For example, both an `int` and a `float` can be 4 or 8 bytes long, but the same series of bits are interpreted in very different ways.

Within the numeric data types, there is also the concept of signed vs. unsigned variables. As their names suggest, signed variables have a sign and the ability to hold negative values, while unsigned ones do not. In a signed variable, the most significant bit holds the sign, while in unsigned variables, this bit is part of the value.

Integer overflow and underflow vulnerabilities are enabled by variables' fixed sizes and the ability to cast a value between signed and unsigned types. Values stored in a variable must remain within a set range, and unsafe casts between variables can cause the same series of bits to be interpreted in different ways.

Integer Overflows

An integer overflow vulnerability occurs when too small of a variable is used to hold a value. For example, a 32-bit unsigned integer can hold values in the range 0 to 4,294,967,295, while 32-bit signed integers can hold values in the range –2,147,483,648 to 2,147,483,647. If a value greater than this maximum value is placed in the variable, the value saved is the value of the 32 least significant bits of the original number.

Integer overflows can occur in one of two ways. One option is that the result of a computation exceeds the maximum value that can fit in a variable. Figure 5.1 illustrates this for an 8-bit value.

```
   1  1  1  1  1  1  1  1
+  0  0  0  0  0  0  0  1
1 |0  0  0  0  0  0  0  0|
```

Figure 5.1: Integer overflow

The other possibility is that an unsafe typecast forces a value into a variable too small to hold it. For example, the value 3000000000 fits into an unsigned integer but not a signed one.

The following code sample is from a smart contract containing an integer overflow vulnerability named batchOverflow by PeckShield.[1]

```
function batchTransfer(address[] _receivers, uint256 _value)
        public whenNotPaused returns (bool){
        uint cnt = _receivers.length;
        uint256 amount = uint256(cnt) * _value;
        require(cnt > 0 && cnt <= 20);
        require(_value > 0 && balances[msg.sender] >= amount);

        balances[msg.sender] = balances[msg.sender].sub(amount);
        for (uint i =0; i < cnt; i++) {
                balances[_receivers[i]] = balances[_receivers[i]].add(_value);
                Transfer(msg.sender,_receivers[i],_value);
        }
        return true
}
```

This code sample is designed to send the same amount of value to multiple recipients. The code calculates the total amount of value to be sent and validates that the sender has at least this much value in their account. Then, it individually transfers value to each of the intended recipients.

This code has a potential integer overflow value in the calculation of $amount$. If the product of cnt and $\_value$ is at least 2^{256}, then the value of $amount$ will overflow. For example, a cnt of 8 and a $\_value$ of 2^{253} will produce a product of 2^{256}, which is more than can fit in $amount$, resulting in a value of 0 being stored in $amount$. An $amount$ of 0 will pass the test `balances[msg.sender] >= amount`, allowing the transfers to go through.

When performing the transfers in the loop, the code uses the variable $\_value$, which indicates the amount to be sent to each recipient. As a result, each recipient will receive a transfer of 2^{253} tokens, while the sender's account is debited 0 tokens (the value of $amount$). These recipients could then later withdraw their balances from the contracts, extracting value that legitimately belongs to other users.

Integer Underflows

Integer underflows exist when a variable is asked to store a value lower than its minimum value. This too can occur as a result of a calculation or due to trying to use the wrong variable type to store a value.

Unsigned variables can only store positive numbers, so any value less than zero will underflow the variable. This could occur as a result of a mathematical operation or due to an unsafe cast from a signed variable, which can store negative numbers.

The following code sample is an example of a withdraw function that contains an integer underflow vulnerability.

```
function withdraw(uint _amount) {
    require(balances[msg.sender] - _amount >= 0);
    msg.sender.transfer(_amount);
    balances[msg.sender] -= _amount;
}
```

In this code sample, the purpose of the `require` statement is to validate that an account contains the requested amount before allowing it to be withdrawn. In theory, subtracting the amount from the balance and testing that the result is nonnegative should work.

However, the variables used in the calculation ($amount$ and $balances$) are both unsigned integers, which means that the result will be an unsigned integer as well. Since unsigned integers cannot store a negative number, the result of the calculation will always be greater than or equal to zero. As a result, the `require` statement will approve any withdrawal request, enabling a malicious user to steal value from the contract.

Countermeasures

Arithmetic vulnerabilities generally result from using the wrong variable type for an operation or an unsafe conversion between variable types. These may be detected by automated tools or should be picked up by a code review.

Case Studies

In December 2021, the PIZZA DeFi project was exploited for $5 million in tokens. The attackers took advantage of an integer overflow vulnerability in the eCurve smart contract to create a massive amount of Tripool tokens.[2] These tokens were then deposited into the PIZZA smart contract, which allowed the attacker to extract the other tokens deposited within the contract.

Decimal Precision

Smart contracts commonly contain mathematical operations, especially when they store and transfer value. One common vulnerable code pattern is division before multiplication.

In Solidity—and any other programming language—numeric data types have limited precision. While this may not matter in most cases, division and multiplication with large numbers can cause small rounding errors to have significant effects.

The following code sample uses a divide-before-multiply code pattern when calculating the value of a token.

```
function calcLiquidityShare(uint units, address token,
    address pool, address member) {
    uint amount = iBEP20(token).balanceOf(pool);
    uint totalSupply = iBEP20(pool).totalSupply();
    return(amount.div(totalSupply)).mul(units);
}
```

Solidity works with integer data types, which means the result of the division will be rounded before the multiplication is performed. This could result in a final answer that is different and smaller than if multiplication were performed before division. As a result, the token is undervalued, and the user receives less in trade than they should.

Countermeasures

When performing multiplication and division in Solidity, use the multiply-before-divide code pattern. This helps to preserve the precision of the result but risks integer overflows.

Digital Signature Vulnerabilities

Digital signatures provide the ability to authenticate a transaction and validate that it has not been modified in transit. Digital signatures are commonly used in smart contracts, especially in the DeFi space.

However, digital signatures can go wrong in a few different ways:

- **Missing Validation:** Digital signatures are useful only if they are validated. Missing signature validation can allow an attacker to submit fake requests on behalf of other users.

- **Cryptographic Errors:** Cryptographic algorithms can be fragile and must be properly implemented to be secure. One example of a cryptographic vulnerability is the reuse of random values across multiple signatures.

- **Malleable Signatures**: In some cases, the data covered by a digital signature may be interpreted in different ways, due to serialization or other factors.

The effects of digital signature errors depend on the vulnerability in question. They range from accepting a forged transaction to providing the attacker with complete control over the account used to generate the signature.

Countermeasures

Digital signatures should be implemented with trusted cryptographic libraries whenever possible. Also, code should ensure that signatures are validated before accepting transactions.

Case Studies

In July 2021, the Anyswap protocol was the victim of a hack due to cryptographic errors in its implementation of the Elliptic Curve Digital Signature Algorithm (ECDSA).[3] Multiple transactions used the same value of K, which is supposed to be a random, single-use value. As a result, part of the signature, R, was identical for both signatures, making this reuse trivial to detect.

With these two signatures, an attacker was able to calculate the private key used in generating the signatures. This gave the attacker control over the blockchain account and the ability to steal an estimated $7,870,000 in tokens.

External Dependencies

The use of library functions and other third-party dependencies is common both for traditional programming and smart contracts. Code reuse can help to expedite the development process and can result in improved code performance and security if high-quality libraries are used.

However, the use of external dependencies makes this third-party code part of an application's attack surface. The following list includes two of the risks associated with external dependencies:

- **Vulnerability Exploitation:** Third-party code may contain vulnerabilities that leave it open to attack. A smart contract with external dependencies may inherit vulnerabilities from this third-party code.

- **Denial-of-Service Attacks:** A smart contract may rely upon external smart contracts and functions to implement important functionality. If these external dependencies become unavailable due to self-destruction or other issues, then a smart contract may be rendered inoperable unless it can be updated to remove these dependencies.

Smart contracts are designed to interact, and minimizing redundant code is especially important on the blockchain because it helps to minimize bloat on the blockchain's digital ledger. However, the use of external dependencies can create security risks for a smart contract.

Countermeasures

External dependencies should be audited before use to identify any potential security issues that they could introduce into a smart contract. Additionally, smart contracts should be deployed in such a way that they can be changed as needed to remove or update vulnerable or deprecated dependencies.

Case Studies

Parity wallet was a smart contract-based wallet. Users of the wallet could deploy their own instances of the contract, which relied on a central library contract for core functionality.

This library function contained an access control vulnerability that allowed an attacker to take ownership of the contract.[4] The attacker then called the contract's `self_destruct` function, which rendered it unusable. Since all Parity wallet contracts relied on this contract for core functionality, this caused the 513,774.16 ETH, plus other tokens stored in these wallets, to be lost forever since the functions needed to transfer these tokens out of the wallets no longer existed.

Right-to-Left Control Character

Right-to-left control characters are a feature in computers that allows them to support different languages. While English is written from left to right, other languages, like Arabic, are written from right to left. Non-printable control characters make it possible to switch between text directions, enabling support for both conventions.

Since these control characters are non-printable and can appear anywhere in a line of text, they can be used by an unscrupulous smart contract developer to obfuscate the meaning of their code. Smart contracts are often open source, building trust by allowing anyone to review a contract's code.

The following code sample was developed by Skylight Cyber to demonstrate the malicious use of right-to-left control characters.[5]

```
contract GuessTheNumber {
  uint _secretNumber;
  address payable _owner;
  event success(string);
  event wrongNumber(string);

  constructor(uint secretNumber) payable public {
    require(secretNumber <= 10);
    _secretNumber = secretNumber;
    _owner = msg.sender;
  }

  function getValue() view public returns (uint) {
    return address(this).balance;
  }

  function guess(uint n) payable public {
    require(msg.value == 1 ether);

    uint p = address(this).balance;
    checkAndTransferPrize(/*The prize*/p , n/*guessed number*/
        /*The user who should benefit */,msg.sender);
  }

  function checkAndTransferPrize(uint p, uint n, address payable
guesser)
    internal returns(bool) {
    if(n == _secretNumber) {
      guesser.transfer(p);
      emit success("You guessed the correct number!");
    }
    else {
      emit wrongNumber("You've made an incorrect guess!");
    }
  }

  function kill() public {
    require(msg.sender == _owner);
    selfdestruct(_owner);
  }
}
```

This code sample is a game where a user places a bet and tries to guess a secret number. If they win, they receive a prize.

The guess function validates that the user has made a bet of 1 ETH and stores the current value of the pot in p. Then, the checkAndTransferPrize function is called, which checks if n equals the secret number and, if so, sends the prize to the winner.

In this contract, the malicious line of code is the call to the checkAndTransferPrize function, as follows:

```
checkAndTransferPrize(/*The prize*/p , n/*guessed number*/
        /*The user who should benefit */,msg.sender);
```

This command sends the prize amount, the guessed number, and the account address of the winner to the checkAndTransferPrize function.

However, the comments in this line of code are not present due to good coding practices. Instead, the comments in the first line of code contain non-printable control characters that switch text direction from left-to-right to right-to-left and back again.

In reality, this code sample tests if the secret number is equal to the value stored in the contract, not the user's guess. Since secretNumber is less than or equal to 10, a contract with a value of at least 11 Ether will be unwinnable. The actual code passes n as the first argument to the checkAndTransferPrize function and p as the second.

However, the use of right-to-left and left-to-right characters make it appear that these arguments are reversed. As a result, a code review provides an inaccurate understanding of the contract's function, which could trick people into wasting money playing an unwinnable game.

Countermeasures

The use of right-to-left and left-to-right control characters for deception is only effective because these characters are non-printable. As long as the resulting source code looks right in a text editor, there is no reason to suspect this attack.

While right-to-left and left-to-right control characters are unprintable, they still exist in the source code of the contract. Scanning for these characters can help to detect this attempted deception.

Unsafe Serialization

Serialization enables data structures to be converted into a string of bits for transmission or storage. At the other end, the recipient unpacks this sequence of bits based on knowledge of the underlying structure. Smart contracts can implement serialization using functions like Ethereum's `abi.encodePacked`.

If a smart contract does not properly validate serialized data, attackers can exploit serialization with deliberately malformed data. One example of this is Smart Contract Weakness Classification (SWC) 133, which addresses hash collisions caused by data serialization with variable-length arguments.

Ethereum's `abi.encodePacked` function can cause serialized data containing arrays to have multiple different interpretations. If packed data contains multiple, adjacent arrays, then values can be moved between these arrays without changing the final serialized value.

If the same serialized data can be deserialized in multiple different ways, then a digital signature authenticating one version can be used to authenticate any of them. An attacker can use this to bypass authentication mechanisms or to perform malicious transactions on another account's behalf.

Ethereum's short address vulnerability is another example of an unsafe deserialization vulnerability. This vulnerability is illustrated in the following code sample.

```
event Transfer(address _from, address indexed _to, uint256 _value);
function sendCoin(address to, uint amount) returns (bool sufficient) {
        if(balances[msg.sender] < amount) return false;
        balances[msg.sender] -= amount;
        balances[to] += amount;
        Transfer(msg.sender, to, amount);
        return true;
}
```

Ethereum serializes inputs to a function, which is unpacked by the called function. If one argument is too short, then it steals the missing byte(s) from the next argument. In the preceding code sample, an attacker can send a value of *to* that is deliberately one byte too short.

The `sendCoin` function does not check the length of *to* and *amount*, so the comparison of *balances* and *amount* uses the correct value of *amount*. However, the `Transfer` function specifies the length of the arguments, so Ethereum right-pads *amount* with zeros, multiplying it by 256. As a result, the value transferred is far higher than the amount approved in `sendCoin`.

Countermeasures

Serialization vulnerabilities are usually caused by serialization of variable-length data or a failure to validate data during the serialization process. The use of fixed-size data structures and validation that serialized data properly unpacks can help to mitigate this vulnerability.

Case Studies

In February 2022, the Superfluid protocol was the victim of a $13 million hack. The attacker took advantage of a serialization vulnerability in how the project tracked state within a transaction across different Superfluid agreements.

The `ctx` variable used for state tracking is intended to be initialized as an empty placeholder by the `callAgreement` function. The attacker included a malicious `ctx` in a call to `callAgreement`, which then added its placeholder to the serialized calldata sent to other agreements.

Since the malicious `ctx` preceded the placeholder one, the target agreements accepted it and ignored the placeholder value. Also, since the calldata came from a trusted contract, the agreement did not validate it. The malicious `ctx` included a forged transfer of tokens from another account to the attacker, which the agreement processed.

Blockchain-Specific Vulnerabilities

Blockchain systems work very differently than traditional software environments. Instead of running on a computer, smart contract code executes on top of the blockchain. The instructions to be executed are embedded in transactions, which are broadcast to the network and organized into blocks before finally being added to the digital ledger and executed.

The unique design of the blockchain creates the potential for smart contract vulnerabilities. The following are examples of vulnerabilities that exist because smart contracts run on top of the blockchain:

- Access control
- Bad randomness
- Denial of service
- Frontrunning
- Rollback attacks
- Time stamp dependence

Access Control

Most smart contract platforms are implemented as open, public blockchains. Anyone can create an account on the blockchain, create transactions, and interact with smart contracts hosted on the blockchain.

However, not all functionality within a smart contract may be intended to be publicly accessible. As a result, smart contract platforms have the ability to restrict access to certain functions, variables, and so on to particular parties, such as the owner of a smart contract.

To restrict certain functionality to particular parties, a smart contract needs to define whom those parties are. Typically, this is done by specifying the address of certain blockchain accounts. While these addresses could be hardcoded into a smart contract, this is not best practice because these addresses may need to be updated when the contract is running.

Many smart contracts have an `initContract` or similar function that assigns ownership after the smart contract is deployed. The following code sample shows an example of an `initContract` function with an access control vulnerability.

```
function initContract() public {
    owner = msg.sender;
}
```

The function is designed to assign ownership of a smart contract to the address that calls the function. Other functions in this contract would then be labeled as only accessible to the contract owner.

This function is designed to be called when the contract is first launched; however, it lacks any restrictions that prevent it from being called multiple times. Instead of assigning ownership of the contract to the first account that calls `initContract`, the function assigns ownership to the account that called it most recently. This could allow an attacker to access privileged functions within the contract, potentially stealing value from it or using its permissions to bypass other access controls.

Countermeasures

This function was vulnerable because it did not prevent multiple calls to it. The following code snippet fixes this issue.

```
function initContract() public {
    require(firstCall);
    owner = msg.sender;
    firstCall = false;
}
```

When this contract is launched, *firstCall* would be set to true, allowing the deployer to claim ownership of the contract. However, after *firstCall* is set to false during the first call to the function, all future calls would fail because the `require` statement would resolve to false.

This example is the simplest way in which smart contract access control mechanisms could fail. Before launching a smart contract, all access control mechanisms should be reviewed for potential vulnerabilities or bypasses.

For example, consider a function designed to only be called from other functions within a smart contract like `privateFunction` in the following code sample.

```
function privateFunction(_data) private {
      // Perform privileged actions
}
function forwarder(address callee, bytes _data) public {
      callee.delegatecall(_data);
}
```

If a public function (like `forwarder`) within the contract makes it possible to call that function with user-controlled arguments, then the function is essentially public as well.

Case Studies

The Poly Network hack is the biggest DeFi attack to date, with over $611 million in tokens stolen. The attacker exploited a chain of trust relationships between various functions within the smart contract move from a publicly accessible one to one with the ability to update the role of keeper within the smart contract.[6] With the access provided by the keeper role, the attacker was able to drain the value stored within the Poly Network project.

Bad Randomness

Random number generation is a common requirement of smart contracts. For example, many games implemented as smart contracts exist that need to generate random numbers to identify winners.

However, random number generation is difficult on the blockchain for a couple of reasons:

- **Determinism:** For the "world computer" to work, every node in the network needs to be able to run the same code and get the same result. If each node independently generated pseudorandom numbers when running contract code, nodes would fall out of consensus regarding the state of the "world computer."

- **Public Ledger:** All transactions are publicly visible on the blockchain's digital ledger, including those creating and calling smart contracts. As a result, nothing is private on the blockchain.

Smart contracts have used different methods of generating pseudorandom values, but many of these are insecure. Some of the most common approaches are as follows:

- **Secret Values:** Smart contract code may be deployed with a secret value used to seed a pseudorandom number generator (PRNG). However, since transactions are public on the blockchain, anyone can read the secret value and predict the sequence of pseudorandom values.

- **Secret Code:** Instead of using a secret seed and a known PRNG, a smart contract developer may create their own function for generating pseudorandom numbers. However, since smart contract code is deployed within a transaction and publicly visible, this has the same issues as secret values.

- **Blockchain Metadata:** Some smart contracts try to use unpredictable blockchain metadata, such as the time stamp or hash value of a block. However, some of these values are manipulable by a block producer, and all are also accessible to other smart contracts as well.

The following code sample includes weak random number generation.[7]

```
function play() public payable {
        require(msg.value >= 1 ether);
        if (block.blockhash(blockNumber) % 2 == 0) {
                msg.sender.transfer(this.balance);
        }
}
```

In this function, the source of randomness is the hash of a particular block. While the value of *blockNumber* is not shown, no option provides a strong random number:

- **Current Block:** The hash of the current and any future blocks is unknown, so the value defaults to 0. This means that a value of *blockNumber* pointing to the current block would always result in a win.

- **Over 256 Blocks Ago:** Solidity only stores the hashes of the previous 256 blocks, and requests for older blocks produce a value of 0. As a result, a *blockNumber* more than 256 blocks ago would be an automatic win.

- **Recent Blocks:** For any of the last 256 blocks, another smart contract could access the block hash and test if it is a winner. If so, it could call the *play* function only when guaranteed to win.

Countermeasures

Any information within the blockchain ecosystem that is available to one smart contract is likely available to another. The only way to generate a secret random value is to do so from outside the blockchain ecosystem.

Smart contracts should use an external oracle to provide randomly generated values. Since every node in the network would see the same value from the oracle, this enables determinism without using values accessible to other, malicious smart contracts.

Case Studies

The SmartBillions lottery was a betting game hosted on the Ethereum blockchain. Players could choose six lucky numbers and then call the won function to play. If their lucky numbers matched a random number when they called won, then they could earn increasing rewards.

SmartBillions's random number was based on the hash of an earlier block, which is only accessible for the previous 256 blocks in Solidity. The attacker guessed lucky numbers of zero and called won 256 blocks after the target block, guaranteeing that their guess would be correct.[8] They were able to win 400 ETH from the game before the creators used a backdoor to drain the remaining 1,100 ETH from the contract.

Denial of Service

Blockchain systems are designed to be distributed and decentralized. No node in the network is essential, which means that the blockchain system lacks permanent single points of failure. In theory, this should provide strong protection against denial-of-service (DoS) attacks.

In practice, blockchain systems and the smart contracts that run on them are vulnerable to DoS attacks in various different ways, including the following examples:

- **DDoS against Transaction Creator:** For a transaction to execute a smart contract, it needs to be broadcast to the blockchain network by its creator. If a DDoS attack renders the creator of a transaction unable to publish it, then it will not be added to the ledger.

- **DDoS against Block Producer:** Transactions are only added to the ledger and executed as part of blocks. If a block producer cannot create a block, then transactions are delayed from being added to the ledger.

- **Transaction Flooding DDoS:** Blockchains create blocks with a fixed maximum size at regular intervals, which means they have a maximum throughput. If a blockchain is flooded with spam transactions, then legitimate transactions may not be able to get through and be added to the digital ledger.

- **Eclipse/Routing Attacks:** Transactions and blocks are distributed via the blockchain's peer-to-peer network. If these messages are intercepted and dropped by an attacker, then they may be delayed or prevented from being added to the digital ledger.

- **Malicious Block Creators:** Block producers have full control over which transactions are included in the blocks they create. A block producer can choose not to include a transaction within a block, delaying it from being added to the digital ledger.

Once a transaction has been distributed to nodes, it should be included in a block eventually unless all block producers collude to prevent this. However, some smart contracts are time-dependent, so delaying a transaction calling them could have a significant impact on the result.

Countermeasures

Many of these attacks target the underlying infrastructure that the blockchain relies upon. Traditional DDoS attacks or attacks on the connectivity of the blockchain network are IT security problems that can be addressed with traditional solutions. However, the decentralization of the blockchain network might make it difficult to have these solutions universally adopted, such as having all block producers deploy DDoS protection.

Other DoS attacks exploit the design of the blockchain, such as transaction-flooding attacks and the potential for malicious block creators. Transaction flooding could be mitigated by block producers ignoring spam transactions, and in the absence of universal collusion by block producers, a legitimate transaction may be delayed but will eventually be included in a block.

Case Studies

Sia is a decentralized, blockchain-based storage system. In June 2021, a multi-day DDoS attack against the network targeted a quarter of Sia network hosts and storage providers.[9] While the attack was unable to impact file storage operations, it did interrupt 30 percent of host connections.[10]

Frontrunning

Transactions are not immediately added to the blockchain's digital ledger. After a transaction is created, it is broadcast to all blockchain nodes via the peer-to-peer network. Each node then stores the transactions to be included in a later block. Only when a transaction is included in a block is it executed and added to the digital ledger.

This design provides opportunities for an attacker to see a transaction and create one of their own based on it before the first transaction is processed. In fact, since transactions are typically added to blocks in order of their transaction fees, an attacker can create a transaction with a higher fee that is likely to be processed before the original one.

This ordering of transactions based on fees is referred to as miner extractable value (MEV), and the ability to exploit it is the basis for frontrunning bots. Figure 5.2 illustrates how these bots can take advantage of frontrunning vulnerabilities for profit.

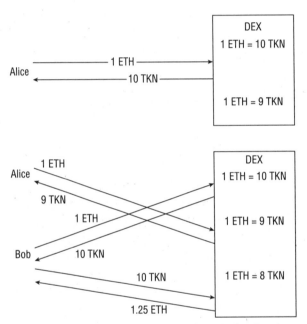

Figure 5.2: Frontrunning attack on a decentralized exchange

A decentralized exchange (DEX) is a cryptocurrency exchange implemented as a smart contract. DEXs need to be able to calculate the exchange rate of various trading pairs. Often, they are implemented based on the laws of supply and demand: the more the DEX has of a particular asset, the lower its relative value.

In the top half of the image, Alice performs a trade with the DEX. Since the exchange rate is currently 1 ETH for 10 TKNs, sending 1 ETH to the contract returns 10 TKNs. Since the DEX's supply of ETH grows relative to its supply of TKN, the relative value of ETH decreases compared to TKN.

The bottom half of the image illustrates a frontrunning attack on this trade. While Alice still sends in 1 ETH, Bob observes the transaction and frontruns it with his own transaction. As a result, Bob makes a trade at the original exchange rate of 1 ETH:10 TKN, while Alice's trade is made at the reduced exchange rate of 1 ETH:9 TKN.

After Alice's trade is complete, Bob makes another trade, exchanging his 10 TKN for ETH. Since the two previous trades increased the value of TKN relative to ETH, Bob gets 1.25 ETH in return. As a result, he makes a net profit of 0.25 ETH, minus the fees for his two transactions.

This is one example of how frontrunning can be used to benefit an attacker. A frontrunner may also be able to win contests based on a first-come-first-served model.

Countermeasures

Frontrunning attacks take advantage of the design of the blockchain, where block producers have full control over how transactions are organized into blocks. A block producer is expected to organize transactions based on associated fees but may also choose to prioritize certain transactions, enabling them to frontrun transactions without fees.

Smart contracts can be designed to minimize the risk or benefit of frontrunning. For example, a contract could randomly pick a winner from the first x submissions rather than operating on a first-come-first-served model. While an attacker could create many frontrunning transactions to defeat this system, it is more expensive, potentially making it unprofitable.

Case Studies

The DODO DEX and Punk Protocol are DeFi projects that were targeted by attacks in 2021. While these attacks did not involve frontunning, the attackers' transactions were frontrun by automated bots. By copying the attacker's transaction and paying a higher transaction fee, these bots exploited the vulnerable contracts before the attacker did, draining some of the targeted funds.

In both cases, the owners of the frontrunning bots were able to limit the impact of the attack. The Punk Protocol bot operator returned $5 million worth of tokens,[11] while the DODO DEX bot operator returned $1.88 million in tokens.[12]

Rollback Attacks

Most smart contract platforms take an all-or-nothing approach to transactions by default. If any part of a transaction fails, then the entire transaction is rolled back.

An attacker can take advantage of this when interacting with a smart contract like a blockchain-based game. A smart contract can call the game contract, and if it doesn't like the result, it could revert the transaction. This would mean that the attacker only plays if they will win anyway.

Countermeasures

Rollback attacks have the greatest impact if a rolled-back transaction triggers another transaction that goes through. Whenever possible, smart contracts should only initiate new transactions after verifying that transactions triggering them executed successfully.

Case Studies

In December 2018, Betdice, EOSMax, Tobet, and other EOS-based gambling apps were the victims of a rollback attack.[13] The attacker performed transactions from an address blacklisted by the block producer, which meant that it would never be accepted and included within a block.

However, servers associated with the gambling apps saw and processed the transaction and determined that it would win the game. They then initiated transactions sending a reward to the player. As a result, the attacker's initial betting transactions were not recorded on the blockchain, but the reveal transactions containing their reward were.

Time Stamp Dependence

Some smart contracts may be designed to take action at a certain point in time. For example, a contest may open at midnight January 1, so submissions before that time would be rejected while ones after would be accepted.

Smart contracts rely on time stamps within the block header for the current time. However, this is not a reliable clock. Block header time stamps are under the control of the block producer and have a high degree of flexibility. For example, the Ethereum Virtual Machine (EVM) only requires that each block have a time stamp greater than that of the previous block. While nodes may reject blocks with time stamps too far into the future, there is no formal definition for a valid time stamp.

This creates the potential for a block creator to manipulate time stamps for their own benefit. For example, the following code snippet has time-stamp-dependent functionality.

```
function play() public {
        require(now > 1521763200 && neverPlayed == true);
        neverPlayed = false;
        msg.sender.transfer(1500 ether);
}
```

This code implements a contest where the first player after time stamp 1521763200 wins 1,500 ETH. A node creating a block shortly before this time could cheat by setting the block time stamp to 1521763201 and including a transaction in the block where they called the `play` function and claimed the reward. As long as their block is accepted by the network, they can win the contest before other users start playing.

Countermeasures

Time-stamp-dependence vulnerabilities exist because time stamps are under the control of the block producer. While some blockchains have constraints on acceptable time stamp values in block headers, these constraints are often flexible to account for unsynchronized clocks and the latency of blocks traveling over the peer-to-peer network.

A better approach to implementing time-dependent functions is the use of block heights rather than block time stamps. These values are not under the control of a block producer and provide a reasonable approximation of the current time. For example, while Bitcoin's blocks aren't created at exactly 10-minute intervals, they are close enough that a certain block height should be reached within a certain window.

Case Studies

GovernMental was a Ponzi scheme smart contract that ran on the Ethereum blockchain. The rules of the game were that, if no one performed a transaction to the contract within 12 hours, the previous player would be awarded the jackpot.

This smart contract could be exploited by an attacker who produced a block close to the expiration of the 12-hour window.[14] By forging the time stamp in the block header, the malicious block producer could force the contract to pay out early, before the 12 hours were complete.

Platform-Specific Vulnerabilities

Smart contract platforms are an extension of the original blockchain protocol. Bitcoin does not support smart contracts, and different smart contract platforms have implemented this functionality in different ways. Smart contract platforms may use existing programming languages and virtual machines or may have created their own.

As a result, different smart contract platforms are prone to different vulnerabilities. Ethereum and EOSIO are two of the oldest and most used smart contract platforms, which means that they have had the most opportunity for these platform-specific vulnerabilities to be discovered.

Ethereum

Ethereum is the oldest smart contract platform, launching July 30, 2015. The age and widespread adoption of this platform provided ample opportunity to identify potential vulnerabilities on the platform. The following list includes some examples of vulnerabilities specific to the Ethereum smart contract platform:

- Denial of service: block gas limit
- Denial of service: unexpected reversion
- Forced send of ether
- Missing zero address checks
- Reentrancy
- Token standards compatibility
- Unchecked return values
- Unsafe external call

Denial of Service: Block Gas Limit

Ethereum uses the concept of gas to fight spam and compensate nodes for their efforts. Gas is a fraction of an Ether, and each instruction in the EVM has an associated gas cost.

When creating a transaction that runs a smart contract, an account will include some gas with it. If that gas runs out before the transactions completes, it is reverted.

Ethereum also has a block gas limit, which caps the amount of gas that can be used within a block. While this has its benefits, it also creates the potential for DoS attacks. If a smart contract function requires more gas than can be included in a block, then it cannot be executed.

The following code snippet shows an example of a function with a DoS vulnerability caused by block gas limits.

```
function selectNextWinners(uint256 _largestWinner) {
       for(uint256 i = 0; i < largestWinner, i++) {
              // heavy code
       }
       largestWinner = _largestWinner;
}
```

This function contains a loop whose number of iterations is determined by the user. The loop runs through some operations based on previous inputs and then assigns the value of _ `largestWinner`, an argument to the function, to `largestWinner`, which determines the loop's termination condition. Inside the loop is heavy code that consumes a significant amount of gas.

This function will be rendered unusable as soon as the value of `largestWinner` grows large enough that execution of the loop meets or exceeds the block gas limit. This could happen intentionally as part of an attack or as part of legitimate usage since the value of `largestWinner` presumably grows as more users play the game.

Whoever triggers this Out of Gas exception will presumably win the game, as no new player would be able to run the `selectNextWinners` function to replace them. As a result, an attacker has incentive to choose a large value of `largestWinner` to render it unrunnable in the future.

Countermeasures   Block gas limit vulnerabilities generally exist in code that has unbounded loops or recursion. In the preceding example, the number of loop iterations was under the control of the smart contract's users. As a result, the function could be placed in a state where it would be impossible to run within the block gas limit.

To avoid this issue, Ethereum smart contracts should avoid unbounded loops or recursion. It is also a good idea to modularize code wherever possible to minimize the amount of gas used by any function. If a sequence of actions can be broken up across multiple transactions, this reduces the probability of hitting the block gas limit.

Case Study   The GovernMental contract mentioned in the Timestamp Dependence case study also included DoS vulnerabilities due to Ethereum's block gas limits. The process that allowed a player to claim the reward also included some cleanup code.

This included two arrays that tracked the state of the contract. Once the array of participants grew past a certain point, attempting to clear it would exceed the block gas limit. As a result, it would be impossible for a player to win the game and claim the reward.[15]

Denial of Service: Unexpected Reversion

In Ethereum, a smart contract account is nearly identical to a normal user account. The only difference is that a smart contract account has code associated with it that can be executed by another account.

As a result, smart contracts have the ability to send, receive, and store value. This is essential to smart-contract-based games and DeFi smart contracts that allow users to deposit and withdraw value within a contract.

One vulnerability associated with value transfers in smart contracts is the potential for a transfer of value to be unexpectedly reverted. If a smart contract sends value to another smart contract, the recipient contract's fallback function will be run, allowing it to execute some code. That fallback function could be designed to revert any transactions to it.

If a smart contract assumes that all transfers will succeed, this can cause a DoS vulnerability within the contract. The following code sample contains an example of this vulnerability.

```
contract Auction {
        address currentLeader;
        uint highestBid;

        function bid() payable {
                require(msg.value > highestBid);

                // Refund the old leader, if it fails then revert
                require(currentLeader.send(highestBid));

                currentLeader = msg.sender;
                highestBid = msg.value;
        }
}
```

This code sample is from the King of the Ether smart contract,[16] which names a monarch and then allows other players to pay to claim the title. When this occurs, the previous monarch receives the payment made by their successor.

In this function, the `require(currentLeader.send(highestBid))` command creates a DoS vulnerability due to the potential for reverted transactions. If the current monarch reverts any transfers to them, then this code will fail.

The intention here was to ensure that the previous monarch always got their payment before they were unseated. However, this code allows a monarch who reverts payments to them to cause any attempt to unseat them to fail.

Countermeasures   This function was vulnerable to DoS attacks because it assumed that all transactions would succeed. Solidity includes a try-catch structure that can be used to handle reversion in external calls, enabling a contract to detect and respond to failed transfers.

Forced Send of Ether

As mentioned previously, unexpected reversion within a fallback function can cause a DoS vulnerability within the calling contract. Forced send of Ether vulnerabilities look at the other side of this and what happens if a contract with a reverting fallback function is forced to receive Ether.

The following code snippet shows an example of an Ethereum smart contract that attempts to revert all transfers of value.[17]

```
contract Vulnerable {
      function () payable {
            revert();
      }

      function somethingBad() {
            require(this.balance > 0);
            // Do something bad
      }
}
```

In Ethereum, fallback functions are labeled by the keyword `payable`. In this contract, all attempted payments are automatically reverted. The reason is that, in the `somethingBad` function, some undesirable event occurs if the contract ever holds a nonzero value.

This contract effectively protects itself against normal transfers of value, such as the use of send in the unexpected reversion example. However, there are a few ways in which an attacker can bypass this, sending Ether to the contract without triggering the fallback function:

- **Prefunding:** Smart contract accounts are like any other account on Ethereum, meaning they can receive transfers before smart contract code is deployed to them. If an attacker can predict the deployment address of a smart contract, then they can transfer Ether to it before the contract is deployed and the fallback function exists.

- **Mining/Staking:** Participating in consensus can result in block rewards. An attacker can indicate that a smart contract account is the intended recipient of a block reward, which does not trigger the fallback function.

- **Self-Destruct:** A self-destructing smart contract can specify another contract as the recipient of any Ether held at that address. Transfers triggered by self-destruct do not trigger the recipient's fallback function.

Using one of these methods, an attacker can force Ether into the target smart contract. In this case, a future call to `somethingBad` would pass the `require` statement, allowing the bad functionality to execute.

Countermeasures   Forcing Ether into a smart contract is usually only a problem if the contract performs strict value comparisons. For example, the command `if (value == 5)` is problematic if an attacker forces 6 ETH into the contract.

Instead of using strict value comparisons, contracts should use greater than or equal to or less than or equal to. This way, any unexpected Ether does not break the contract's functionality.

For code where strict tracking is necessary, such as the previous toy example, value should be tracked internally rather than via `this.balance`. The following code sample shows an example of this.

```
contract Fixed {
        function () payable {
                if (isAcceptableTransaction()) {
                        balance = balance + msg.value;
                } else {
                        revert();
                }
        }

        function somethingBad() {
                require(balance > 0);
                // Do something bad
        }
}
```

In this example, only value transfers that pass through the fallback function will affect the value of `balance`. As a result, forced sends of Ether will not trigger the `somethingBad` function.

Case Studies   The Edgeware project allowed users to lock ETH in 3 to 12 months in exchange for a reward. When a user created a lockdrop, the main Lockdrop contract created a new contract that held their ETH and implemented the lock functionality. These contracts were vulnerable to forced send of Ether because they asserted at creation that the value of the contract was strictly equal to the amount of ETH sent in by the user.[18]

The Lockdrop contract used a deterministic algorithm to determine the address of the next contract. Since the address of the new contract was predictable, an attacker who prefunded the address with ETH could cause the creation of the lock contract to fail. Also, since the Lockdrop contract would keep trying to use the same address until it succeeded, locking the next address would cause it to fail forever.

Missing Zero Address Checks

The genesis, or zero, address (0x0) is used for burning tokens in Ethereum. Since the private key for this address is unknown and likely never to be discovered, tokens sent to this address cannot be recovered.

When working with addresses, it is important to ensure that an address is not the zero address. Transfers of tokens or ownership of a contract to the zero address cannot be reversed.

Smart contracts can also have errors if they assume that smart contract code exists at the 0x0 address. The following code sample shows vulnerable code implements a safeTransferFrom function for a token.[19]

```
function safeTransferFrom(address token, address from,
  address to, uint value) internal {
      (bool success, bytes memory data) =
        token.call(abi.encodeWithSelector(0x23b872dd, from, to, value));
      require(success && (data.length == 0 || abi.decode(data, (bool)),
        "!safeTransferFrom");
}
```

In this code, the safeTransferFrom function is called in the contract that created the deposited token. This should transfer that token from one address to another.

If the address of *token* is the 0x0 address, then the call function will try to call the fallback function of the contract at 0x0, which does not exist. Instead of reverting, this call will succeed, making it appear that a token transfer succeeded when it did not. As a result, the contract will accept and respond to a nonexistent transfer.

Countermeasures   When working with transfers of tokens and calls to smart contracts, a contract should always check for the zero address. Additionally, smart contracts should verify that smart contract code exists at an address before attempting to call functions within it.

Case Studies   The previous vulnerable code sample is from the Qubit project, which implements a bridge between the Ethereum and the BNB Chain platforms. This bridge was hacked in January 2022.

The attacker took advantage of a missing zero address check to trick the bridge into accepting a fake deposit of ETH, which triggered a Deposit event. This event was caught by the bridge's smart contract, which caused qxETH tokens to be minted to the attacker's account on BNB Chain, which the attacker converted into $80 million in BNB.

Reentrancy

Reentrancy is likely the most famous Ethereum-specific vulnerability. It was the cause of the DAO hack, which was the most significant Ethereum hack to date.

Like unexpected reversion, reentrancy is made possible by the ability to execute code within a fallback function. The following code snippet contains a reentrancy vulnerability.

```
function withdraw(uint _amount) {
        require(balances[msg.sender] >= _amount);
        msg.sender.call.value(_amount)();
        balances[msg.sender] -= _amount;
}
```

This `withdraw` function checks to see if a withdrawal request is valid, transfers the value to the target address, and then updates its internal ledger accordingly. However, the command `msg.sender.call.value(_amount)()` executes before this state update and allows a target smart contract to execute some commands.

A malicious smart contract can exploit this vulnerability by calling the `withdraw` function again from inside its fallback function. Assuming that the account has a balance of 5 ETH and is requesting a withdrawal of 4 ETH, this would produce the following sequence of events:

- Malicious contract calls `withdraw` function.
- `require` statement validates that the transaction is valid (5 >= 4).
- Vulnerable `withdraw` function t sends 4 ETH to malicious contract, triggering fallback function.
  - Malicious contract calls `withdraw` function.
  - `require` statement validates that the transaction is valid (5 >= 4).
  - Vulnerable `withdraw` function sends 4 ETH to malicious contract, triggering fallback function.
  - Fallback function returns.
  - Vulnerable contract updates internal state (`balances[msg.sender]` = 1).
  - Vulnerable `withdraw` function returns.
- Vulnerable `withdraw` function updates internal state (`balances[msg.sender]` = -3).
- Vulnerable `withdraw` function returns.

Because the vulnerable `withdraw` function only updates its internal state after performing the value transfer, an attacker can make multiple calls with the original value of `balances[msg.sender]`, allowing them to extract excess value from the contract. The number of reentries is largely limited by the amount of gas available at each iteration.

Countermeasures   Reentrancy vulnerabilities can be eliminated by following the check-effects-interaction code pattern. This involves the following:

- **Check:** Check that a request is valid (i.e., the `require` statement from the example).
- **Effects:** Record the effects of the event (i.e., updating the value of `balances[msg.sender]`).
- **Interaction:** Perform the action (i.e., transferring the value).

With this code pattern, the reentrant call to the `withdraw` function would have failed at the `require` statement because `balances[msg.sender]` would equal 1, not 5.

Case Studies   The DAO hack is the most famous Ethereum hack to date. The DAO was a contract designed to implement crowdfunding on the blockchain. Project proposals could be submitted to the contract and voted on by DAO token owners. If approved, they would receive funding, and successful projects would pay dividends to DAO token holders.

A reentrancy vulnerability in the DAO smart contract allowed the attacker to drain value from the contract by repeatedly requesting a withdrawal before the contract updated its internal state.[20] The attacker stole approximately 3.6 million ETH from the contract.

In the end, the DAO hack was ultimately unsuccessful because the Ethereum network performed a hard fork that rewrote history to erase it from the ledger. This sparked the division of the Ethereum (ETH) and Ethereum Classic blockchains, which contain the nodes that did and did not follow this hard fork. This broke the rules of blockchain immutability but helped preserve the value of ETH.

Token Standards Compatibility

Ethereum has a number of standards called Ethereum Improvement Proposals (EIPs). Among these is the EIP-20 standard that specifies a standard interface for tokens created on the Ethereum smart contract platform.[21]

EIP-20 specifies function prototypes for common token functions, including their arguments, return values, and required actions such as firing certain events. However, not all tokens follow the EIP-20 standard.

For example, EIP-20 specifies that `transfer` and `transferFrom` functions return a Boolean value indicating success or failure. However, the USDT stablecoin returns `void` in these functions.

This can cause incompatibility with smart contracts that strictly follow the EIP-20 standard like the following command:

```
require(IERC20(inputToken).transfer(msg.sender,_amountIn),errorMessage);
```

The use of `require` here means that a compliant token will allow continued execution if transfer succeeds and causes reversion if the transaction fails. However, transactions that call this code with a noncompliant token like USDT will revert every time because `require(null)` will throw an error.

Countermeasures   Projects like OpenZeppelin have implemented `safeTransfer` and `safeTransferFrom` functions that properly handle both return value checks and noncompliant tokens. Using these implementations provides both security and support for noncompliant tokens.

Case Studies   ForceDAO was a DeFi aggregator project that was hacked for $367,000 in tokens within hours of launch.[22] The project's vaults were a fork of the xSUSHI contract, which was vulnerable to tokens that did not comply with the EIP-20 standard.

An attacker deposited tokens into the contract that would return false rather than reverting upon a failed deposit. Since the contract did not check return values, it issued xFORCE tokens due to these failed deposits. The attacker could then redeem these xFORCE tokens for FORCE tokens stored in the contract's vault.

Unchecked Return Values

In Solidity, functions can indicate failure in a couple of different ways. If a low-level function reverts, then this can cause the transaction to be completely rolled back unless handled by a `try-catch` block. However, if a function indicates failure by returning false, then the calling function can continue execution at its next command.

This difference in how low-level functions handle errors can create smart contract vulnerabilities, like the one in the following code sample.

```
function withdraw(uint256 _amount) public {
        require(balances[msg.sender] >= _amount);
        balances[msg.sender] -= _amount;
        etherLeft -= _amount;
        msg.sender.send(_amount);
}
```

The preceding code sample implements a withdraw function with reentrancy protections. The crucial line of code here is the use of the `send` command to send value.

Solidity defines a few different mechanisms for sending Ether to another contract:

- `transfer`: Costs 2300 gas and indicates failure by throwing an error
- `send`: Costs 2300 gas and indicates failure by returning false
- `call`: Sends an arbitrary amount of gas and indicates failure by returning false

The `send` and `transfer` functions are nearly identical except in how they handle errors. In the previous code sample, if something goes wrong with the call to `send`, the transfer may fail without detection because the contract is not checking the return value. This could leave the contract in an invalid state because it has already recorded the transfer in its *balances* and *etherLeft* variables.

Countermeasures   The example vulnerability existed because a function failed to check for failure in a call to another function. This issue could be fixed by researching how a particular function handles errors before using it or assume the worst and implement error-checking functionality for all calls to external functions.

Case Studies   An earlier version of the King of the Ether contract mentioned previously contained an unchecked return value vulnerability.[23] The contract did not include enough gas with a call to send to support transfers to a smart-contract-based wallet, which would execute a fallback function. As a result, an attempt to refund the previous monarch failed when that monarch used a smart-contract-based wallet.

Since the contract did not check the return value of the call to send, the failure was ignored and the throne was transferred to the next claimant. However, when this was discovered, the contract operators extracted the value from the contract and sent it to the previous monarch.

Unsafe External Call

In Ethereum, a smart contract account is no different from a user account, and smart contracts are designed to interact with one another. However, the ways in which a smart contract function calls other functions has a dramatic impact on its security.

The following code sample implements a call forwarder and is an example of unsafe calls to external functions.

```
contract Proxy {

  address owner;

  constructor() public {
    owner = msg.sender;
  }

  function forward(address callee, bytes _data) public {
    require(callee.delegatecall(_data));
  }
}
```

Solidity's `delegatecall` function enables a smart contract's functions to be called while maintaining the context of the calling function. The code executed within the callee has access to the caller's data and value, and any calls made by the callee with have `msg.sender` set to the caller's address.

By using `delegatecall`, a smart contract is placing complete trust in the called function. The callee can modify or delete the caller's data, steal value from the caller, and bypass access controls by masquerading as the caller when calling other functions.

Countermeasures   Never use `delegatecall`. Anything that can be done using `delegatecall` can be done more safely another way.

Case Studies   Furucombo is a drag-and-drop interface for DeFi traders to build chains of trades. Furucombo allowed users to preapprove transfers for certain tokens, enabling the contract to extract these tokens from the user's account without explicit approval.

Furucombo's `batchExec` function allowed a `delegatecall` to the Aave proxy contract.[24] This allowed the attacker to call the Aave contract's fallback function, which performs a `delegatecall` to its implementation logic contract. The attacker exploited this chain of `delegatecalls` to have the implementation contract set to their own malicious contract.

Using this same chain of `delegatecalls`, the attacker can then call functions in their own contract using the state of the Furucombo contract. The attacker can then transfer preapproved tokens from users' accounts to their own.

EOSIO

EOSIO is another early example of smart contract technology that has been used to host various distributed applications (DApps). The following list includes some examples of vulnerabilities particular to the EOSIO platform:

- Fake tokens
- Notification assumptions
- Reentrancy
- Unchecked transaction status

Fake Tokens

In many smart contract platforms, token names and symbols must be unique. An attempt to create a new token with the same symbol as an existing token will fail.

On EOSIO, different smart contracts can create tokens with the same symbols. This can lead to fake token vulnerabilities like that in the following code sample.[25]

```
void test::transfer(name from, name to, asset quantity, string memo)
{
  if (from == _self)
  {
    // we're sending money, do nothing additional
    return;
  }

  eosio_assert(to == _self,"contract is not involved in this transfer");
  eosio_assert(quantity.symbol.is_valid(),"invalid quantity");
  eosio_assert(quantity.amount > 0,"only positive quantity allowed");
  eosio_assert(quantity.symbol == EOS_SYMBOL,"only EOS tokens allowed");
}
```

The test::transfer function in this code sample performs validation that a transfer is valid before accepting it. This includes validating that the token symbol is EOS, the native token of EOSIO.

However, in EOSIO, the combination of contract and symbol is unique, not just the token symbol itself. This function would accept a transfer of any token with a symbol of EOS, not just the official EOS token. This could allow an attacker to deposit a worthless token and extract tokens with actual value from the contract.

Countermeasures   In EOSIO, the combination of a token contract and symbol is unique, not just the token symbol. When validating a transfer, it is necessary to check that both of these match expected values.

Case Studies   The BitDice project contained a fake token vulnerability that was exploited in October 2019.[26] The code verified that a token symbol matched EOS but not that the token contract matched `eosio.token`. As a result, an attacker was able to send fake EOS tokens from the contract and then extract 4,000 real EOS tokens from it.

Notification Assumptions

In EOSIO, smart contracts can receive notifications about particular events and create listeners that execute code if they receive these notifications. The most common notification is when a user is involved in a transaction either as sender or receiver.

The following code sample is vulnerable to exploitation due to incorrect assumptions about how notifications work in EOSIO.[27]

```
void transfer(uint64_t sender, uint64_t receiver) {

  auto transfer_data = unpack_action_data<st_transfer>();

  if (transfer_data.from == _self ||
      transfer_data.from == N(eosbetcasino)){
   return;
  }

  eosio_assert( transfer_data.quantity.is_valid(), "Invalid asset");
 }
```

This transfer function is designed to act when it receives a transaction. It is triggered by a notification about a transfer and tests whether it was the one that initiated the transfer. If not, it assumes that it is the recipient of the transaction and responds accordingly.

The problem with this code is that any EOSIO account can be notified about a transaction using the `require_recipient` command. This function could be tricked by an attacker who performs a transfer between two other accounts and notifies this one via `require_recipient`.

In this case, the contract will correctly determine that it was not the source of the transaction. However, it will then wrongly conclude that it was the recipient, which may result in it sending tokens to an attacker or taking other action in response to the deposit that it believes it received.

Countermeasures   With `require_recipient`, anyone can be notified of a transfer or other event. When responding to a notification about a transfer, it is necessary to verify that the contract was in fact the recipient of the transfer and not just that it is not the sender.

Case Studies   The vulnerable code sample previously shown is from the EOSBet casino smart contract, which was exploited in October 2018.[28] The attackers sent transfers from account ilovedice123 to whoiswinner1 while notifying the EOSBet casino contract using `require_recipient`. Since EOSBet did not verify that it was the recipient of the transaction, it credited the transfer to the attacker's account.

Reentrancy

Reentrancy vulnerabilities exist in Ethereum because fallback functions allow third-party, potentially malicious code to be run between adjacent instructions of a calling function. EOSIO contracts are also vulnerable to reentrancy, but it works differently.

The following code sample demonstrates a reentrancy vulnerability.[29]

```
[[eosio::on_notify("*::transfer")]]
void tester::on_transfer(const name from, const name to,
  const asset quantity, const string memo )
{
  log_action log( get_self(), { get_self(), "active"_n });
  log.send( "hello from " + get_self().to_string() );
}
```

In EOSIO, reentrancy vulnerabilities originate from the notification system. As mentioned previously, EOSIO allows smart contracts to be notified of certain events via `require_recipient`, and these notified contracts can execute code when they receive these notifications.

This handler code may include *inline actions* such as the log action in the preceding sample. Logically, it would seem that this inline action would be executed immediately after the `on_transfer` function.

However, EOSIO executes all notification handlers for an event before it will run any inline actions. This means that the log action in the preceding code may execute long after the `on_transfer` function with code from other functions in between.

This creates the potential for reentrancy attacks if a vulnerable contract splits operations between notification handlers and inline actions. For example, a contract might perform a transfer in the handler and then use an inline action to perform a state update or vice versa. An attacker that can split these two actions may be able to exploit the contract.

Countermeasures   Reentrancy attacks in EOSIO take advantage of the fact that inline actions are not immediately executed after the notification handler that triggers them. Whenever possible, make actions and state updates atomic rather than splitting them over notification handlers and inline actions.

Case Studies   In May 2021, the Vaults.sx yield aggregator smart contract was the victim of a reentrancy attack.[30] The attack included the following steps:

1. Attacker deposited tokens in exchange for SX tokens.

2. The attacker redeemed half of these SX tokens.

3. When notified of the redemption transaction, the attacker created two inline actions. One triggered Vault.sx's update function, while the other redeemed the other half of its SX tokens.

4. When notified of the redemption transaction, the vault.sx contract created an inline action to pay out rewards and updated its internal total supply value based on this update.

5. The attacker's inline actions executed, overwriting the balance update in step 4, which had not yet executed.

6. The attacker received redeemed tokens. The second redemption included excess rewards because it was based on an incorrect value of the contract's total supply.

Unchecked Transaction Status

In EOSIO, a transaction can have several different statuses,[31] including the following:

- `executed`: Transaction succeeded, and no error handling was executed.

- `soft_fail`: Transaction failed but error handing succeeded.

- `hard_fail`: Transaction and error handling failed.

- `delayed`: Transaction delayed by user to execute in the future.

- `expired`: Transaction expired, and CPU/NET was refunded to the user.

For most of these, the behavior of EOSIO is logical. Successful transactions are recorded on the chain, while unsuccessful or expired ones are not.

The exception here is delayed transactions. When a transaction is delayed, its contents are recorded on the blockchain. Later, when the delay timer expires, nodes can extract the contents of the transaction from a block to execute and validate it.

Delayed execution is not a problem if a transaction succeeds. However, a delayed transaction that results in a status of `hard_fail` is still recorded on the blockchain.

This can create confusion for smart contracts that observe transactions but do not validate their status. A smart contract may see that a transaction to it exists on the blockchain and respond accordingly. However, this transaction may be delayed and designed to result in a `hard_fail`, meaning that it did not actually execute. As a result, the vulnerable contract has reacted to a transaction that never happened.

Countermeasures   A transaction's `status` is one of the fields within a transaction receipt. Smart contracts should check this field and verify that it has a status of executed before accepting a transaction.

Case Studies   Vegas Town contained an unchecked transaction status vulnerability that was exploited by fortherest12 in March 2019. The attacker used delayed transactions to send transfers to the contract that would result in a status of `hard_fail` but still be recorded on the blockchain. The vulnerable contract failed to check the status of these transactions, causing it to accept failed transactions.

Application-Specific Vulnerabilities

Smart contracts can be used for various different purposes. Two of the main applications of smart contracts today are decentralized finance (DeFi) and non-fungible tokens (NFTs).

Both of these applications of smart contracts introduce features and functions that do not exist in all smart contracts. With them come potential vulnerabilities and security issues unique to these use cases.

DeFi Vulnerabilities

Bitcoin was designed to implement a decentralized financial system using the blockchain's digital ledger. However, Bitcoin is largely designed to track transfers of value on the blockchain.

DeFi smart contracts are designed to implement other functions of financial institutions, such as borrowing, lending, and making exchanges between assets. These smart contracts are extremely valuable but can also contain various vulnerabilities:

- Access Control
- Centralized Control
- Frontend Vulnerabilities
- Price Manipulation

Access Control

Access control vulnerabilities can exist in any smart contract. However, the unique nature of the DeFi space creates new types of access control vulnerabilities, and the high value of DeFi contracts exacerbates their impacts.

In DeFi contracts, mint and burn functions must be appropriately protected. The following code sample shows an unprotected mint function.[32]

```
function mint(address to, uint256 amount) public virtual {
        mint(to, amount);
}
```

DeFi smart contracts commonly have a native token. These tokens may be designed to indicate ownership of a share of the contract's liquidity (which could accrue interest) or issued when a user takes out a loan to allow them to reclaim their collateral.

A mint function like the one in the preceding code allows new tokens to be created. An unprotected one could allow an attacker to create new tokens and send them to their account. In the sample code, the mint function is labeled as public, meaning that anyone can call it to create new tokens.

If this occurs, the existing tokens lose some value, and the attacker can steal value from the protocol. For example, minting 100 tokens when 100 exist would cut the value of each token in half but allow the attacker to claim half of the value invested in a DeFi contract.

A burn function does the opposite, destroying some of a smart contract's native tokens. If an attacker can burn tokens held by a contract, then the remaining tokens gain additional value. If an attacker holds these tokens, they can extract more value from the protocol than they put in.

Countermeasures   Access control best practices for DeFi contracts are the same as for smart contracts in general. Functions should be labeled as private by default and only be made publicly accessible if necessary for the smart contract's logic.

Case Studies The Zenon Network was the victim of a hack in November 2021.[33] An unprotected `burn` function allowed anyone to destroy wZNN tokens held by the contract.

The attacker deposited tokens into the contract to earn wZNN, then burned over 26,000 wZNN tokens. This caused the value of wZNN tokens to increase significantly because the value held by the contract mapped to fewer wZNN tokens. The attacker was then able to extract over $1 million in WBNB by redeeming their wZNN tokens.

Centralized Control

Access control vulnerabilities exist when too many people have access to high-risk functions within a smart contract. However, implementing strong access control can also create security risks for a contract by centralizing control of that contract's protected functions.

Many DeFi contracts are deployed using a single signature wallet, which means that only one private key is necessary to sign transactions that access private functionality such as `mint`, `burn`, and `self_destruct` functions. This makes it easier for an attacker or a malicious insider to take over the contract and steal the value that it contains.

The following code sample is an example of a centralized control vulnerability.[34]

```
function mint(uint256 amount) public onlyOwner returns (bool) {
    _mint(_msgSender(), amount);
    return true;
}
```

This `mint` function correctly limits access to minting functionality, making it more difficult for an attacker to mint unauthorized tokens. However, there are no restrictions on the owner's ability to mint new tokens, meaning the contract owner could mint new tokens at will, devaluing those held by other users. This functionality could be abused by the owners of the contract or exploited by an attacker who gains access to the account of the contract's owner.

Countermeasures Access management is important to DeFi security, but privileged access should be decentralized as much as possible. All DeFi contracts should be managed by multisignature wallets, which require access to multiple private keys to perform privileged functions.

Ideally, DeFi smart contracts should operate under a decentralized governance model that does not put full control in the hands of the project team.

This can help to protect against *rug pull* attacks where project members drain value invested in a project and disappear.

Case Studies   The bZx DeFi protocol lost over $55 million in tokens in a November 2021 hack.[35] The attackers exploited the fact that the smart contract was not using a multisignature wallet.

A phishing email to a bZx developer installed malware that stole the private keys for both the developer's personal accounts and the ones that managed the bZx contract. The attacker then used these keys to drain funds from the developer's account, the bZx contract, and any bZx users who had preexisting approvals for tokens on bZx.

Frontend Vulnerabilities

Most DeFi protocols are not implemented solely as a smart contract. They also have a web frontend that provides a user-friendly interface for interacting with the smart contract. This distributed application (DApp) architecture works similarly to traditional web applications, except that backend systems are implemented as a smart contract on the blockchain rather than an application on a web server.

Frontend applications should be part of the threat model for DeFi smart contracts. Some frontend security risks are as follows:

- **Malicious Scripts:** Compromised frontend systems may have malicious JavaScript injected into a page. The JavaScript could attempt to steal private keys or create malicious transactions for users to unwittingly approve.

- **Interface Mismatch:** Mismatches in the interface between the web frontend and smart contract backend can create unintentional and undesired effects. For example, actions performed on the frontend may not be passed on to the smart contract backend and recorded on the blockchain.

- **Account Takeover:** Users typically authenticate to web frontends with a username and password, and these sites may store and manage private keys. An attacker who steals a user's password via phishing or other means could access their private key and take over their blockchain account.

- **Denial-of-Service Attacks:** Web frontends are a single point of failure in a DeFi project. A DDoS attack against these sites could render a project inaccessible to legitimate users.

These are only some of the security risks associated with a web frontend for a DeFi project. These sites combine the traditional security risks of web applications with those associated with smart contract security.

Countermeasures   DeFi projects' web frontends are like any other website. They should be analyzed for potential vulnerabilities and business logic errors as part of the security audit process.

Case Studies   Users of the BadgerDAO smart contract were hacked using a frontend exploit in December 2021.[36] The attacker inserted malicious JavaScript into the project's web frontend that inserted approvals for sending tokens to the attacker's address in transactions generated by users. Over 500 wallets made these unwanted approvals, which the attacker used to drain over $120 million in tokens from them.

Price Manipulation

Price manipulation vulnerabilities are some of the most common attacks in the DeFi space. They are made possible by on-chain calculations of tokens' values and the existence of *flashloans*.

Typically, when a borrower takes out a loan, they need to provide some collateral. This collateral is an asset with a value roughly equal to the amount of the loan. If the borrower defaults on the loan, the lender can seize this asset to recoup their losses.

Collateral is necessary in traditional finance because it allows lenders to manage their risk. In DeFi, flashloans can be made without collateral because a lender can make risk-free loans.

This is possible because of how transactions work in the blockchain. In many blockchains, transactions are all or nothing. If part of a transaction fails, the entire transaction is rolled back as if it never happened.

Flashloans take advantage of this by requiring that a loan taken at the start of a transaction be paid back by the end of that transaction. If the borrower defaults and does not make this repayment, then the whole transaction is invalidated and the loan never happens. As a result, lenders can make huge, risk-free loans because these loans are always paid back by the end of a transaction.

Some DeFi smart contracts calculate the exchange rates of various tokens based on supply and demand and the value of the contract. The following code sample includes a calculation of the value of a DeFi contract's native token.[37]

```
function calcLiquidityShare(uint units, address token,
   address pool, address member) {
```

```
uint amount = iBEP20(token).balanceOf(pool);
uint totalSupply = iBEP20(pool).totalSupply();
return(amount.mul(units)).div(totalSupply);
}
```

This function calculates the share of a smart contract's liquidity that a user can claim by depositing some of the contract's native tokens. With flashloans, an attacker can manipulate this calculation by inflating the asset balance of the contract relative to its quantity of native tokens. This allows the attacker to drain value from the contract by redeeming its overvalued tokens.

Countermeasures Price manipulation exploits take advantage of on-chain calculations of a token's value. Contracts can avoid slippage by using Chainlink or similar price oracles.

Case Studies In October 2021, Cream Finance was exploited for over $130 million in tokens.[38] The attack began with a flashloan and included a loop of depositing tokens into Cream and using the deposit as collateral for another borrow. One of the attacking contracts accrued approximately 1.5 billion in crYUSD and ~500 million in yUSDVault tokens.

The attacker deposited the yUSDVault tokens to extract yUSD and decrease the total supply of tokens in the vault to $8 million. A deposit of $8 million in yUSD then doubled the vault's total supply and the perceived value of crYUSD tokens. The attacker was able to use its now roughly $3 billion in crYUSD tokens to pay off its flashloans and extract $130 million from the vault.

NFT Vulnerabilities
Tokens hosted on a smart contract platform can be divided into two main categories:

- **Fungible:** Tokens are completely interchangeable. For example, a dollar bill is fungible because one bill has the same value as another.

- **Non-Fungible:** A particular token has a unique, inherent value. For example, one baseball card might be worth much more than another despite the fact that they are both ink on paper.

In blockchain, non-fungible tokens (NFTs) can be used to perform blockchain-based tracking. For example, the most common application of NFTs today is to track ownership of digital art. However, NFTs can also be used for logistics, identity management, and other purposes.

NFTs have a lot of potential, but they also have security issues. Some of the major security concerns of NFTs today are as follows:

- Forged NFTs
- Malicious NFTs
- Off-Chain Asset Storage
- Platform Centralization
- Unconstrained Token Supply

Forged NFTs

NFTs are designed to track ownership of an asset on the blockchain. This ownership can then be transferred by sending the NFT between wallets. However, NFTs are based on the assumption that the creator of the NFT actually owns the asset and has the right to create the NFT.

Currently, most NFTs are supposed to track ownership of digital artwork. Forged NFTs are created without the knowledge and consent of the artist or current owner of the artwork, meaning that they have no inherent value.

Countermeasures   Validating the authenticity of NFTs is difficult because it likely requires verification of the asset by its owner. However, performing background research on an NFT offering may help with determining if it seems legitimate or suspicious.

Case Study   In March 2021, artist Derek Laufman learned that a verified profile impersonating him on the Rarible NFT marketplace was selling NFTs of his art without his knowledge.[39] Although Rarible took the account down after it was brought to their attention, at least one fan had already bought an NFT of his work.

Malicious NFTs

Most modern NFTs are designed to track ownership of digital art. To view the art, a user needs to follow the link embedded in the NFT, which makes them an ideal vehicle for phishing attacks.

Malicious NFTs could be designed to use social engineering to trick users into handing over their credentials for an NFT platform like OpenSea or the private key of their blockchain account. If successful, the attacker could then use this access to steal tokens and NFTs from the user's account.

Countermeasures   Malicious NFTs are image files that contain malicious code. Scanning image files for such code before opening them can help to protect against this attack.

Case Study   In October 2021, Check Point Research discovered vulnerabilities in OpenSea that would allow for malicious NFTs attacks.[40] Carefully crafted CVG files could be used to create pop-ups that would prompt the user to take actions that could reveal their credentials or private key. There is no indication that this vulnerability was exploited, and OpenSea remediated it on its platform.

Off-Chain Asset Storage

Blockchains are designed to be immutable digital ledgers, meaning that bloat is a significant concern. Any data stored on the blockchain must be stored indefinitely by every node in the blockchain network.

For this reason, NFTs are not stored directly on the blockchain's digital ledger. Instead, an NFT contains a URL that points to the associated image or the hash of that image on Interplanetary Filesystem (IPFS), a decentralized storage system.

This design means that an NFT does not indicate ownership of a piece of digital art so much as a particular URL or IPFS hash. The image at a particular URL or IPFS hash may be taken down or (in the case of URLs) changed. If this is the case, then the NFT loses its value.

Countermeasures   For owners of NFTs hosted on IPFS, the owner of a token could take over the role of the IPFS gateway that hosts a copy of their NFT. However, URL-based NFTs could be taken down or replaced with another file at any time.

Case Study   Multiple NFT platforms have taken down forged NFTs that infringed on the rights of the real owners of the content. For example, Cent shut down sales of many NFTs in February 2022 due to "rampant fakes and plagiarism."[41]

Platform Centralization

While NFTs are stored on the blockchain, most users interact with them via a web frontend. This makes managing NFTs more convenient but also introduces new vulnerabilities.

These NFT platforms are centralized and introduce the same vulnerabilities as DeFi web frontends. Attackers could take down a website with a DDoS attack or embed malicious content in it to steal users' private keys or NFTs.

Countermeasures   As in the DeFi space, frontend vulnerabilities should be addressed during a security audit. This includes testing for web application vulnerabilities in the web frontend and validating the business logic of the frontend, backend, and interfaces between them.

Case Study   In January 2022, OpenSea users were the victims of a hack that exploited miscommunications between the platform's web frontend and smart contract backend.[42] Users believed that they were delisting NFTs when they were transferred between wallets because they were no longer listed for sale on the web frontend. However, these transactions were not recorded in the smart contract backend. An attacker sent transactions directly to the smart contract to buy these tokens at earlier sale prices well under the market rate.

Unconstrained Token Supply

Many modern NFTs are instances of generative art, where an algorithm puts together sets of building blocks in various different ways. Many NFT collections derive at least some of their value from the fact that only a certain number of the NFTs exist in the collection. The scarcity of the asset drives up the value.

However, not all NFT smart contracts enforce these limits. The following code sample is a function from the Bored Apes Yacht Club (BAYC) contract,[43] a popular NFT collection.

```
function reserveApes() public onlyOwner {
        uint supply = totalSupply();
        uint i;
        for (i = 0; i < 30; i++) {
                _safeMint(msg.sender, supply + i);
        }
}
```

This `reserveApes` function allows the owner of the BAYC to mint 30 new NFTs whenever they choose. By updating the URI indicated by the function, they could also add 30 new images to the collection.

Like `mint` functions in DeFi, this runs the risk of devaluing existing NFTs. This would likely either cause these tokens to lose all value or allow the contract owner to create and sell valuable NFTs at will. This vulnerability could be triggered by the contract creator or an attacker exploiting an access control vulnerability.

Countermeasures   NFT minting contracts should have built-in controls that limit the quantity of NFTs within a collection. If expansions are expected in the future, they should be governed by code that prevents unauthorized changes.

Threat Modeling for Smart Contracts

Vulnerabilities in smart contracts can be mapped to all categories of the STRIDE threat model, as in the following examples:

- **Spoofing:** Smart contract vulnerabilities can be used for spoofing in various ways. For example, Solidity's delegatecall allows a malicious contract to masquerade as another contract, and signature vulnerabilities can allow forged transactions to be accepted or even reveal private keys.

- **Tampering:** Reentrancy and `delegatecall` vulnerabilities allow an attacker to tamper with the internal state of vulnerable smart contracts.

- **Repudiation:** Rollback attacks allow an attacker to undo actions before their results are recorded on the digital ledger.

- **Information Disclosure:** Exposure of private keys due to signature errors could allow an attacker to decrypt encrypted messages intended for a user. Also, many bad randomness vulnerabilities are based on the public visibility of information that the contract wished to be private.

- **Denial of Service:** Many denial-of-service vulnerabilities exist in smart contracts, such as Ethereum's block gas limits and unexpected reversion vulnerabilities.

- **Elevation of Privileges:** Access control vulnerabilities give an attacker privileged access to protected functions within a smart contract.

Blockchain Extensions

Smart contracts build on the basic blockchain protocol and have dramatically expanded its functionality. With applications like DeFi, blockchain has expanded from a decentralized system for tracking financial transactions to a fully functional financial system.

However, the capabilities of smart contracts are limited by the infrastructure that they run on. For example, blockchains like Ethereum have relatively low transaction rates (15 per second). This limits the number of transactions that can be performed on this platform and the scalability of the system.

Layer 2 protocols are built on top of Layer 1 blockchains (Ethereum, Bitcoin, etc.) and expand their functionality and scalability. Some common layer 2 protocols are as follows:

- State channels
- Sidechains and bridges

State Channels

A state channel is a Layer 2 protocol that creates a direct payment channel between two blockchain accounts. State channels are set up and taken down by transactions recorded on the blockchain's digital ledger, but all intermediate transactions are performed off chain. Well-known examples of state channels include Bitcoin's Lightning Network and Ethereum's Raiden Network.

At any point in time, both parties in a state channel have a signed commitment from the other about the current allocation of funds in the channel. A channel is set up by creating these mutual commitments and sending the balance stored in the channel to an address that locks it until the channel is closed.

Payments are performed by exchanging new versions of these commitments that reallocate the funds within channel. The channel can be closed if one or both parties publish a mutually signed commitment as a transaction on the blockchain.

If a user unilaterally closes the channel, the other participant has a set period of time in which to submit a more recent version of the commitment. If this occurs, then the defrauded party receives the full balance of the channel. If not, the timelocked funds are unlocked and distributed based upon the published commitment.

State channels allow payments between parties that lack a direct channel between them. This is accomplished by routing payments through a series of channels that link the two parties. These transactions are crafted so that the balance updates with intermediate parties are only approved once the recipient acknowledges receipt of the transaction. Additionally, intermediate channel providers may charge a fee for the use of their channels.

State Channel Security Considerations

State channels rely on many of the same security assumptions as other blockchain technologies, such as the security of digital signature algorithms.

However, the use of state channels also introduces other potential security risks:

- Denial-of-service attacks
- Timelock exploits

Denial-of-Service Attacks

State channels can only process payments if a route exists between the two parties that has sufficient liquidity. For example, Alice can't send 1 Bitcoin to Bob if the current balance of value in their channel only allocates 0.9 BTC to her.

Attackers can take advantage of this fact to perform denial-of-service (DoS) attacks on a state channel network. If an attacker can perform a DoS attack against crucial nodes in a state channel network or unbalance state channels, they can prevent value from being transferred to/from a particular user.

Timelock Exploits

State channels can be closed unilaterally by one of the channel participants. However, a timelock exists on the closure, which can allow the other participant to generate a punishment transaction that allows them to claim the value in the channel.

However, this transaction must be submitted and processed within the timelock to take effect before funds are released. If this transaction is delayed due to an eclipse/routing attack, malicious miner, and so on, then the victim can lose funds.[44]

Sidechains

Every blockchain protocol has its advantages and limitations. For example, Bitcoin has robust security due to a massive amount of hashpower supporting its Proof of Work consensus algorithm. However, Bitcoin has limited throughput and no support for smart contracts. Other blockchains may have greater scalability and smart contract support but lack the security and name recognition of Bitcoin.

Sidechains attempt to address these issues by creating relationships between different blockchains. These links allow users to send tokens to a locking address on one blockchain and have an equivalent number of tokens released on another.

Sidechains can be implemented in a few different ways:

- **Bridges:** Bridges enable links between independent blockchains. For example, Anyswap, Binance Bridge, and Wormhole are examples of major bridges.

- **Child Chains:** Child chains are blockchains that add scalability and features to a blockchain. They have their own methods of creating and validating blocks but use the parent blockchain to resolve disputes. Plasma creates child chains for the Ethereum blockchain.

Sidechain Security Considerations

Sidechains enable interoperability between different blockchains via a mediator. This design creates potential security concerns:

- Centralized bridges
- Independent chain security
- Interface errors
- Vulnerable bridges

Centralized Bridges

A bridge linking two sidechains creates a high degree of centralization. Its users rely solely on the bridge to transfer assets between the two chains.

This degree of centralization creates significant security risks. A denial-of-service attack against the bridge could render it inaccessible to users, or an attacker could exploit the bridge to steal tokens from users or manipulate their value.

In February 2022, the Meter.io bridge was the victim of an attack that exploited an incorrect assumption in how the bridge handled wrapped tokens.[45] By exploiting this vulnerability, the attackers were able to make fake deposits into the bridge and then withdraw real tokens.

This vulnerability decreased the value of BNB.bsc on the BNB Chain. This allowed attackers to buy this token at low rates and use it as collateral for loans from Hunter Finance, which used Chainlink's prices for the asset.[46] Although some of these loans were repaid, the project lost $3.3 million.

Independent Chain Security

Sidechains create links between blockchains, but each blockchain has its own security. For example, a peg between Bitcoin and another chain does not grant the sidechain Bitcoin's protection against 51% attacks.

If a sidechain is the victim of a 51% or other attack, this can affect the exchange rate of tokens between the two chains. This occurred in the Meter.io hack where BNB.bsc was devalued on BNB Chain.

Interface Errors

In theory, a bridge between sidechains will allow users to lock tokens on one blockchain, which will unlock tokens on the other. However, this exchange might not work as designed, especially if the bridge contract contains exploitable vulnerabilities.

This was the case in the hack of Qubit's QBridge in January 2022.[47] A vulnerability in the bridge's smart contract on the Ethereum blockchain enabled an attacker to trick it with a fake deposit of WETH. The bridge accepted the fake deposit and released qXETh tokens for the attacker on BNB Chain.

Vulnerable Bridges

Some links between sidechains are implemented as smart contracts that monitor operations on one blockchain and respond to them accordingly. If these smart contracts contain exploitable vulnerabilities, an attacker may be able to exploit these vulnerabilities to steal tokens from a bridge contract or disrupt its operations.

The hack of the Wormhole bridge in February 2022 was the second most expensive DeFi hack at the time, allowing the attacker to steal $326 million in wETH from the bridge. The attacker exploited a signature verification vulnerability, which involved tricking the contract into believing that a signature had been successfully verified when it had not.[48] This allowed the attacker to mint 120,000 ETH tokens, which they then "legitimately" withdrew from the bridge contract.

Threat Modeling for Blockchain Extensions

Attacks against state channels and sidechains can be mapped to several STRIDE threat categories:

- **Tampering:** Timelock exploits allow an attacker to delete part of the history of a state channel.

- **Repudiation:** Timelock exploits in state channels can allow an attacker to undo transactions performed in these channels.

- **Denial of Service:** Denial-of-service attacks on state channels or bridges can impact accessibility to legitimate users.

- **Elevation of Privileges:** Vulnerabilities in bridge code could grant an attacker control over transfers between sidechains.

Conclusion

Smart contracts and blockchain extensions dramatically extend the functionality of blockchain protocols but also create additional complexity and risk. Most attacks against blockchain systems occur at these levels as attackers take advantage of design flaws or implementation errors in the protocols and programs.

This concludes our exploration of vulnerabilities and security risks at the various levels of the blockchain ecosystem. The next chapter discusses best practices for securely designing, implementing, and auditing blockchain-based systems.

Notes

1. https://peckshield.medium.com/alert-new-batchoverflow-bug-in-multiple-erc20-smart-contracts-cve-2018-10299-511067db6536

2. https://twitter.com/PizzaProFi/status/1468869822389768192

3. https://medium.com/multichainorg/anyswap-multichain-router-v3-exploit-statement-6833f1b7e6fb

4. www.parity.io/blog/a-postmortem-on-the-parity-multi-sig-library-self-destruct

5. https://skylightcyber.com/2019/05/12/ethereum-smart-contracts-exploitation-using-right-to-left-override-character

6. https://slowmist.medium.com/the-root-cause-of-poly-network-being-hacked-ec2ee1b0c68f

7. https://dasp.co

8. www.reddit.com/r/ethereum/comments/74d3dc/smartbillions_lottery_contract_just_got_hacked

9. https://sia.tech/ddos2021

10. https://hacked.slowmist.io/en/search

11. https://medium.com/punkprotocol/punk-finance-fair-launch-incident-report-984d9e340eb

12. https://dodoexhelp.zendesk.com/hc/en-us/articles/900004851126-Important-update-regarding-recent-events-on-DODO

13. https://slowmist.medium.com/roll-back-attack-about-blacklist-in-eos-adf53edd8d69

14. https://eprint.iacr.org/2016/1007.pdf

15. https://eprint.iacr.org/2016/1007.pdf

16. https://github.com/kieranelby/KingOfTheEtherThrone/blob/v1.0/contracts/KingOfTheEtherThrone.sol

17. https://consensys.github.io/smart-contract-best-practices/attacks/force-feeding

18. https://medium.com/@nmcl/gridlock-a-smart-contract-bug-73b8310608a9

19. https://blocksecteam.medium.com/when-safetransfer-becomes-unsafe-lesson-from-the-qbridge-security-incident-c32ecd3ce9da

20. https://medium.com/swlh/the-story-of-the-dao-its-history-and-consequences-71e6a8a551ee

21. https://eips.ethereum.org/EIPS/eip-20

22. https://blog.forcedao.com/xforce-exploit-post-mortem-7fa9dcba2ac3

23. www.kingoftheether.com/postmortem.html

24. https://cmichel.io/replaying-ethereum-hacks-furucombo

25. https://cmichel.io/eos-1-3-contract-development-toolkit-updates

26. www.reddit.com/r/eos/comments/9fpcik/how_eosbet_attacked_by_aabbccddeefg

27. https://github.com/slowmist/eos-smart-contract-security-best-practices/blob/master/README_EN.md#transfer-error-prompt

28. https://blog.peckshield.com/2018/10/26/eos

29. https://cmichel.io/eos-vault-sx-hack

30. https://cmichel.io/eos-vault-sx-hack

31. https://developers.eos.io/welcome/v2.1/protocol-guides/transactions_protocol

32. https://twitter.com/RugDocIO/status/1451067795140005891

33. https://twitter.com/peckshield/status/1462165620506742784

34. https://letmeape.medium.com/how-to-spot-a-potential-rug-clear-signs-something-is-sketchy-169fb84c7084#59e7

35. https://bzx.network/blog/prelminary-post-mortem

36. https://rekt.news/badger-rekt

37. https://peckshield.medium.com/the-spartan-incident-root-cause-analysis-a0324cb4b42a

38. https://rekt.news/cream-rekt-2

39. www.theverge.com/2021/3/20/22334527/nft-scams-artists-opensea-rarible-marble-cards-fraud-art

40. https://gizmodo.com/gullible-opensea-users-were-vulnerable-to-malicious-nft-1847850437

41. www.reuters.com/business/finance/nft-marketplace-shuts-citing-rampant-fakes-plagiarism-problem-2022-02-11

42. https://decrypt.co/91076/opensea-exploit-sees-bored-ape-yacht-club-nft-sell-1700

43. https://etherscan.io/address/0xbc4ca0eda7647a8ab7c2061c2e118a18a936f13d#code

44. www.coindesk.com/tech/2020/10/27/4-bitcoin-lightning-network-vulnerabilities-that-havent-been-exploited-yet

45. https://twitter.com/ishwinder/status/1490227406824685569

46. https://rekt.news/meter-rekt

47. https://certik.medium.com/qubit-bridge-collapse-exploited-to-the-tune-of-80-million-a7ab9068e1a0

48. https://twitter.com/samczsun/status/1489044939732406275

CHAPTER 6

Considerations for Secure Blockchain Design

Blockchain systems face security threats at every level of the blockchain ecosystem. Everything from the underlying cryptography to the smart contracts running on top of the distributed ledger can be attacked in various ways.

However, not all blockchains are created equal, nor are they equally vulnerable to attack. In this chapter, we explore some key factors to consider when designing a blockchain system, including the types of blockchain, privacy and security enhancements, and legal and regulatory considerations.

Blockchain Type

Bitcoin, the original blockchain, was designed as a platform that was universally accessible and fully decentralized. Anyone could create a Bitcoin account, and all accounts could participate in any aspect of the blockchain's operations, such as ledger storage and block creation.

Since Bitcoin, new models for blockchain have emerged that use the same underlying technology but move slightly away from the ideals of full decentralization. Now, blockchains can be classified as public versus private and as open versus permissioned.

Public vs. Private

Public blockchains like Bitcoin and Ethereum are designed to be globally accessible, allowing anyone to create an account on the blockchain. However, this model is not ideal for all use cases, especially for organizations looking to take advantage of the benefits of blockchain technology for their internal operations.

The distinction between public and private blockchains defines who has the ability to create an account on a blockchain platform and create transactions. Public blockchains are openly accessible, while private ones are available only to certain authorized users or from specific networks or systems.

Benefits of Public vs. Private Blockchains

Public and private blockchains both have their advantages and disadvantages, making them each better suited to different use cases. The following list includes some of the advantages of public blockchain platforms:

- **Anonymity:** In a public blockchain, there is no need to determine whether a user is authorized to use the platform. This makes it possible to have anonymous accounts where identity management and authentication are based on knowledge of an account's private key.

- **Decentralization:** Public blockchains allow anyone to create an account, which results in a larger userbase and greater decentralization. Also, limiting access to only authorized users, which is necessary for private networks, requires a system to permit or deny access, which can create a single point of failure.

- **Resiliency:** Public blockchains tend to be larger and more distributed than private ones. This provides a greater degree of resiliency because cyberattacks, natural disasters, and other disruptive events are less likely to impact all nodes within the blockchain network.

Private blockchains are often a better choice for enterprise use cases. Here are some of the benefits that a private blockchain provides:

- **Access Management:** A private blockchain allows an organization to manage who has access to the blockchain system. This provides greater control over the data and functionality hosted on the blockchain.

- **Data Privacy:** On a public blockchain, all users have full visibility into the transactions on the distributed ledger. Private blockchains allow an organization to limit access to the data stored on the ledger.

- **Efficiency:** Private blockchains tend to be smaller than public ones. As a result, they have less redundancy and inefficiency.

- **Regulatory Compliance:** Data protection regulations commonly require organizations to control access to sensitive data and protect it in certain ways. This is easier to accomplish with a private blockchain where the organization has complete control over the network.

Open vs. Permissioned

In addition to the distinction between public and private blockchains, blockchains can be differentiated based on the permission granted to various users. For example, open blockchains put user accounts on an equal footing, where any account can do anything, while permissioned blockchains grant special privileges to certain accounts.

Benefits of Open vs. Permissioned Blockchains

Open and permissioned blockchains have both their pros and their cons. Here are some of the benefits of an open blockchain:

- **Decentralization:** Open blockchains allow any node to participate in all aspects of the blockchain's operations. This provides greater decentralization than private blockchains, where only a subset of nodes can perform certain functions.

- **Simplicity:** Implementing multiple privilege levels requires additional complexity to prevent access controls from being bypassed. Open blockchains are usually less complex than permissioned ones, which decreases the probability of design or implementation errors.

- **User Privacy:** Permissioned blockchains may require knowledge of users' real-world identities to assign the appropriate permissions. Open blockchains allow anonymous accounts, which protects user privacy.

Building permissions and privileges into a blockchain has the following advantages:

- **Access Management:** Permissioned blockchains allow an organization to build access controls into the blockchain. This provides greater control over user access and privileges.

- **Data Control:** Open blockchains allow all users full access to all aspects of the blockchain. Permissioned blockchains make it possible to restrict access based on privilege levels.

- **Regulatory Compliance:** Data protection regulations often require an organization to control access to protected data. Permissioned blockchains make this easier to implement on the blockchain.

Choosing a Blockchain Architecture

Blockchains can be any combination of public versus private and open versus permissioned. For example, the Enterprise Ethereum Alliance (EEA) supports the deployment of private instances of the Ethereum blockchain. Other, public blockchains include master nodes or other privileged accounts in a publicly accessible blockchain.

The selection of the right type of blockchain for a given application depends on the use case and the various security trade-offs. In some cases, the increased decentralization and resiliency of an open and public blockchain might be worth the greater exposure of potentially sensitive information on the ledger. In others, regulatory requirements might mandate strict control over sensitive data, in which a private and permissioned blockchain is the only viable option.

Privacy and Security Enhancements

One of the biggest critiques of blockchain technology is lack of privacy. The design of the blockchain means that the source, destination, and value of every transaction is publicly visible.

However, using additional cryptographic algorithms, it is possible to conceal all of this information and improve users' privacy without breaking blockchain decentralization and nodes' ability to validate transactions before accepting them. Privacy coins like Monero use zero-knowledge proofs, stealth addresses, and ring signatures to conceal the value, destination, and source of blockchain transactions.

Zero-Knowledge Proofs

Zero-knowledge proofs (ZKPs) are constructs that allow someone to prove knowledge of a secret without revealing the secret itself. For example, imagine that you want to prove to a friend who has colorblindness that two otherwise identical balls are the same color without revealing which ball is which color.

To do so, you could give both balls to the friend and have them hide them from you. They would then show you one ball, conceal it, and then again show you one ball. After doing so, they would ask if they were the same ball.

If the balls are in fact different colors, you could differentiate between them with perfect accuracy. If not, there is a 50 percent chance of guessing correctly. By repeating this process many times, it would be possible to decrease the probability of repeated lucky guesses to statistical improbability, proving that the balls are different colors. However, even after an infinite number of trials, the friend still does not know which ball is which color.

ZKPs can be used for various purposes, such as proving knowledge of a password. On the blockchain, a ZKP can demonstrate that a particular account has the balance required to perform a transaction without revealing the transaction or account balance. This makes it possible to implement decentralized transaction validation by blockchain nodes while improving data privacy on the blockchain.

Stealth Addresses

On the blockchain, the source and destination address of every transaction is publicly visible. This enables decentralized validation of transactions because value received in one transaction will be used to fund a later one. Verifying that an account contains the necessary balance to perform a transaction requires the ability to look back to these past transactions.

Stealth addresses are single-use addresses for receiving transactions on the blockchain. These single-use addresses are derived from the user's address, and the owner of the address can derive the private key for these addresses from their private key. This allows them to digitally sign transactions from this address.

Stealth addressing improves privacy because it makes it infeasible for an attacker to determine that a stealth address is associated with a user's account. Also, it is infeasible to determine if two transactions to different stealth addresses are sent to the same user. However, blockchain nodes can validate transactions because transactions from these single-use addresses will be digitally signed with the appropriate private key.

Ring Signatures

Stealth addresses protect the identity of the recipient of a transaction. Ring signatures provide a level of anonymity to the sender of a transaction.

Blockchains use digital signatures to verify the authenticity of a transaction. However, validation of a digital signature requires the public key that matches the private key associated with that account. This reveals the identity of the transaction signer.

Ring signatures make it possible to digitally sign data as a group. Ring signatures enable a user to generate a digital signature that verifies that the signer was the owner of one of a set of public keys, without revealing which one.

Ring signatures work because they require knowledge of a set of public keys and the private key associated with one of those public keys. Since public keys are public and revealed alongside digital signatures, it is easy for a user to collect a set of decoy public keys to use within a ring signature. However, since a private key is required as well, a ring signature validates that the signer is a member of the group.

Legal and Regulatory Compliance

Blockchain technology has received significant attention from businesses ranging from small startups to major enterprises. Blockchain's design and the unique benefits that it provides offer promising alternatives to traditional ways of doing business.

However, a major challenge for companies wishing to adopt blockchain technology is aligning it with their legal and regulatory responsibilities. The regulatory landscape has evolved rapidly in recent years as the passage and enactment of the European Union's General Data Protection Regulation (GDPR) has inspired the creation of similar laws in other jurisdictions.

Blockchain technology offers many benefits and can even be an asset in some aspects of regulatory compliance due to its immutable digital ledger. However, blockchain can also be a source of compliance headaches for various reasons:

- **Data Control:** Data privacy laws commonly mandate that an organization demonstrates control over data protected under the law. For public blockchains, an organization surrenders all control once a transaction is broadcast to the blockchain network.

- **Data Privacy:** Blockchain's digital ledgers are designed to be transparent to enable decentralized transaction validation. This conflicts with organizations' responsibilities to keep certain data private.

- **Encryption Requirements:** Regulations mandate that data be protected with strong encryption. The immutability of the blockchain ledger and potential life spans of blockchain platforms may mean that sensitive data would be exposed if encryption algorithms are broken.

- **Immutable Ledger:** The blockchain's digital ledger is designed to be immutable. This conflicts with the requirements of the GDPR and similar regulations that mandate the deletion of certain data once it is no longer needed for its original purpose.

- **Jurisdictional Boundaries:** Some regulations, such as the GDPR, restrict transfers of their constituents' data across certain jurisdictional boundaries. Many blockchains have global footprints, meaning that sensitive data in blockchain transactions could cross these boundaries.

- **Regulatory Changes:** Regulatory requirements are changing rapidly, so compliant implementations may be noncompliant in the near future. Blockchain decentralization, ledger immutability, and other factors can make it difficult to adapt to changing requirements.

Blockchain technology has the potential to drastically improve corporate processes across various metrics. However, blockchain-based systems are not always the right tool for the job, and security, regulatory, and legal implications are all important factors when considering a blockchain-based solution.

Designing Secure Blockchains for the Future

Blockchain technology is rapidly evolving and is still in its early stages. Today, it is impossible to tell which smart contract platforms will gain mainstream adoption and if blockchain will turn out to be a passing fad or the basis for the future of technology.

Blockchain security evolves along with the blockchain. Some attacks and vulnerabilities may become obsolete as technology changes and new attacks emerge. For example, Chapter 1 of this book predates many of the attacks referenced in the case studies of later chapters.

No book can provide a comprehensive description of all possible blockchain vulnerabilities and attack vectors, but hopefully this one provided foundation and background needed to get started. To keep up with the latest vulnerabilities and hacks, check out blockchain platforms' vulnerability pages, the news, and social media.

Index